MEMORY

MEMORY

HOW IT WORKS

AND

HOW TO IMPROVE IT

by Roy A. Gallant

FOUR WINDS PRESS   NEW YORK

51530 b

Library of Congress Cataloging in Publication Data

Gallant, Roy A
  Memory.

  Includes index.
  1. Mnemonics.   I.   Title.
BF385.G24   153.1'4   79-6342
ISBN 0-590-07613-2

Published by Four Winds Press
A division of Scholastic Magazines, Inc., New York, N.Y.
Copyright © 1980 by Roy A. Gallant
All rights reserved
Printed in the United States of America
Library of Congress Catalog Card Number: 79-6342
5 4 3 2 1 84 83 82 81 80

For Bette, in memory

ACKNOWLEDGMENTS

The quotations describing Dr. Wilder Penfield's work are from *Proceedings of the National Academy of Science*, Volume 44, and from "Memory Mechanisms," by W. Penfield, *A.M.A. Archives of Neurology and Psychiatry*, 67. My thanks for permission to include a brief excerpt from *Invention, Discovery, and Creativity*, by A. D. Moore, © 1969 by Doubleday & Company, Inc.; and for permission to use several excerpts from *The Mind of the Mnemonist*, by A. R. Luria, Avon Discus Books, 1968. The brief excerpt dealing with eidetic images in children is from "Eidetic Images," by Ralph Norman Haber, *Scientific American*, April 1969. The excerpts from Cicero and *Ad Herennium* are from *The Art of Memory*, by Frances A. Yates © 1966 by Frances A. Yates, University of Chicago Press. My special thanks to the late Dr. Bette van Laer, Department of Psychology, Long Island University, for reading the manuscript of this book and for her numerous and helpful comments. Her recent death, before the publication of this book, came as a deep personal loss. A gifted teacher and scholar, she will be missed by friends and colleagues alike.

CONTENTS

"A great and beautiful invention is memory, always useful both for learning and for life."
—from the Dialexeis, c. 400 B.C.

PREFACE

Most people who read a book about memory want to improve their memory. This book is designed to help you do just that. It is also designed to teach you how your memory works. With an understanding of how memory works you will be less likely to expect your memory to perform impossible tasks. But by applying the memory techniques described in this book you will find yourself performing feats of memory that you never thought possible before—and having fun doing it.

Here are some of the major ideas in this book:

1. Each of us has two major memories: "short-term" memory for the temporary storage of information; and "long-term" memory for the permanent storage of information.

2. Our short-term memory has a limited capacity, and when it is full, nothing more can be crammed into it.

3. Our long-term memory has a near infinite capacity to store information, a much greater capacity than any of us ever makes use of.

4. The more material we pack into our long-term memory, the easier it seems to be to store still more material. In short, memory seems to improve with use.

5. It is extremely important for us to organize the material that we want to remember.

6. The better the system we have for organizing material to be remembered, the faster and more efficiently we are able to catalog and file material in our long-term memory.

7. A well-organized long-term memory enables us to do two important things: learn and memorize new material efficiently, and retrieve information quickly.

8. "Rehearsal" is an important means of transferring material from our short-term memory into our long-term memory.

9. Our ability to pay attention and concentrate on new material increases our ability to memorize the material.

10. Translating the material to be remembered into striking and unusual visual images is an important memory technique.

11. "Chunking" is an important way of expanding our short-term memory. It involves regrouping information; for example, regrouping 2 8 3 4 9 6 into the three "chunks," 28, 34, and 96.

MEMORY

1

TESTING
YOUR
MEMORY

This was young Jamie's first trip outside of the United States. He was with his older brother, Jon, and his father, who was driving their small rented car along a narrow English country road. All three were too interested in the scenery to do much talking, other than to call attention to a building or some other feature of the countryside that struck them as being unusual.

On reaching the top of a long hill, they saw, less than a kilometer away, a typical English village built sometime during the late 1700s. Jamie, who had had an interest in architecture since he was fourteen, suddenly leaned forward and placed his hand on his father's arm. "Dad, slow down a bit. There's something about that village, something familiar. It's as though I've been here before, right here on this hill. I know the houses, that church to the left of the village square, and the old inn with the sign of the red lion hanging out front."

"Come on, Jamie," said his brother. "You know you've never been here before. Your mind is playing a trick on you."

"No, it isn't," Jamie insisted. "I tell you I've been here before. In some way I've been here before, but I can't explain how."

Jamie's feeling of having "been here before" is one that nearly all of us have had at one time or another. The experience is so common that it has long had a name, *déjà vu*, which in French means "already seen." Had Jamie been to that village before in some supernatural way? or was his mind playing a trick on him, as his brother suggested? There are at least three possible answers.

One possible explanation of Jamie's experience is that sometime, somewhere, he saw a photograph of an English country village and for some reason it made a strong impression on him. He could have remembered the general layout and characteristic shapes of buildings in the photograph, even the sign in front of the inn. The lion is a very common symbol throughout England, and many inns have signs of a red lion hanging out front. So when Jamie saw the village from the hilltop, he recognized it as something very much like the village in the photograph. Our ability to remember things in a general way, without too many details, can sometimes give us the impression, "I've been here before."

Another possible explanation is that in looking through architecture books or travel ads Jamie had taken a special interest in individual English houses, inns, churches, and other buildings. Then sometime later he had a dream in which he put all the buildings and streets together as a generalized village. As so often happens to us, Jamie did not remember his dream—not until an actual situation very similar to the dream led to the recall of the dream. Psychologists have tested this theory of memory by hypnotizing people. When subjects were under hypnosis, the psychologist described a particular room. Then a few days later the subjects were actually taken into the room described by the psychologist. On entering the room each one reported a strange feeling of having been there before. Supernatural? Spooky? Not at all.

A third possible explanation is that Jamie had seen a photo-graph of the village. Then on seeing the village he recognized it, although he had no recollection of ever having seen the photograph.

I'll never forget that afternoon when as a new college freshman I attended the freshman reception at the president's house. There were about two hundred of us in the freshman class and virtually all of us paid a call on the president and his wife to be welcomed into the college community. After ring-ing the front doorbell I waited, prepared to introduce myself. In a moment the door was opened by the president's wife, and before I could utter a word she smiled pleasantly at me and said, "How nice of you to come, Mr. Gallant, Roy A. Gallant from Portland, Maine. Please do come in and I'll introduce you to some of your new classmates." I had never seen the presi-dent's wife before, nor had she ever seen me, yet instantly she knew my name and where I was from. On talking to numerous other freshmen, I found that each had had the same experi-ence. What a remarkable memory she has, I thought to myself.

Over the years she had developed a technique for training herself to memorize the names and faces of the members of each freshman class by studying their identification cards in the Admissions Office, cards also containing head-and-shoulder photos of each student. We will return to this ability to remember names and faces in Chapter 6, and discover that it really isn't all that remarkable.

Do you have a photographic memory? Chances are that you do not, although some people do. Such people can look at a long table of numbers for a minute or so and then recite the numbers *in any order*, without making an error. Furthermore, some of them can still remember the table months and years later. They have "photographed" the table and have an image of it stored away in their memory. Others who can perform this feat do not "photograph" the table but associate the numbers in such a way that they can long remember the table. According to psychologist Ralph Norman Haber, experiments have suggested that a high percentage (up to 50 percent) of children are born with a photographic memory, but most lose it by the time they reach their early teens.

We will return to the memory feats introduced here and examine them in more detail. When we do, you most likely will find yourself using your memory in a way you have never used it before, *and* being very impressed with what a good memory you can have. Meanwhile, use the three photographs on these pages to give yourself a quick memory test. After you have tried it, give the test to two or three other people, both adults and young people, and compare all the results.

First, study Photo 1 for thirty seconds. Then cover the photograph, close your eyes, and see if you can re-create the photograph. Each time you are able to remember a detail of the photograph write it down on a sheet of paper. A helper would be useful since you would be able to concentrate better and call out details as they come to you. Do this for each of the three photographs, resting for about five minutes between trials. While you are working with one photograph, be sure not to look at either of the other two. You can see at a glance that Photo 2 is more difficult than Photo 1 and that Photo 3 is more difficult than either Photo 2 or Photo 1. If you want to test yourself further in this way you can use photographs in magazines. If you score 95 percent or higher on the third photo, you have an unusually good memory.

Next, study the following series of nine numbers for one minute and see how well you can memorize the series. At the same time notice *how* you are trying to memorize the series:

5 7 4 9 3 8 1 4 7

Third, imagine that you are at a party and your hostess introduces you to Mr. Moskowitz, Ms. Tyler, Mrs. Hustvet, Mr. Romnalley, and Miss Brown. Study these names for one minute and then read on.

Memory-test photo Number 1. See text for instructions and do not study this photograph until you are told to. SCIENCE PHOTO/ GRAPHICS, INC.

It is not uncommon for people fortunate enough to have exceptional memories to realize that their memories are exceptional. Such people usually are admired by their family, teachers, and friends for being easily able to remember telephone numbers, their social security number, names of people they met long ago but have not seen or thought about for many months, batting averages or track times of famous athletes, and so on. A teen-age student taking one of my astronomy courses a few years ago had an exceptionally good memory for numbers and, presumably, for other things. She had no trouble at all quickly memorizing such quantities as the Sun's luminosity (5.6×10^{27} calories per minute), the velocity of light in meters per second to several places (2.99792), or the escape velocity of Saturn (39.4 kilometers per second).

The student's ability to recall these and other numbers with apparent ease led me to suspect that she was an exceptionally intelligent person. But she was not. On examinations that involved her reasoning ability, or her ability to explain the significance of many of the numbers she had memorized, her grades were not much above average. A superior ability to recall names, dates, and other numbers accurately is not necessarily a sign of superior intelligence, any more than winning a state or national spelling bee is a sign of superior intelligence. While memory and intelligence clearly are related in certain ways, people with outstanding memories are not always high scorers on intelligence tests. In Chapter 6 you will find a remarkable example of this point.

EARLY MEMORY SYSTEMS

Try to imagine what it must have been like before the printing press was invented—before there were books and before there were note pads, pencils, and other inexpensive writing materials. In those distant times it was extremely important to have a well-trained memory.

Today few of us make any special efforts to train our

Memory-test photo Number 2. See text for instructions and do not study this photograph until you are told to. WORLD HEALTH ORGANIZATION photo by Paul Almasy.

memories, for we can get by well enough with an untrained memory. If we have forgotten the meaning of a word, we can flip open a dictionary; if we are not sure when James Madison was president of the United States, we look in a history book or an encyclopedia; if we want to know the temperature at which lead melts we look it up in a chemistry handbook. In short, we refer not to the memory areas of our brains for a large amount of the information we need from day to day but to artificial memory banks. In such cases, all we have to remember is how to look for the information we want.

How did teachers, students, orators, and statesmen many centuries ago remember important ideas and other information when they made long speeches? The ancient Greeks invented what came to be called artificial memory, or the art of mnemonics, that enabled anyone to memorize long lists of words or ideas, weighty tables of numbers, quotations from plays, poetry, and essays. So effective was the system that a speaker trained in it could deliver a well-organized talk lasting several hours and not once refer to notes. Actors and dancers have always had to develop mnemonic systems. Imagine the scene at a ballet with the ballerina flying through the air into her partner's arms, but her partner forgetting to be there to catch her.

In brief, most mnemonic systems work on the principle of an organized system of visual images and associations. For example, picture your living room. You are standing in the doorway, say, and looking around the room clockwise. As you do, you see first a chair, then an end table, then a large painting on the wall, the fireplace, another end table, the sofa, and then that cactus plant nearly five feet tall, and so on around the room. The point is that the room is so familiar to you that when you are away from it you can close your eyes and imagine the room in detail.

Now suppose that you have to deliver a talk, without using notes, about skiing. You plan to introduce your talk by describing different snow conditions, then by describing

Memory-test photo Number 3. See text for instructions and do not study this photograph until you are told to. SCIENCE PHOTO/ GRAPHICS, INC.

equipment—skis, boots, poles, and clothing, in that order. Using your living-room memory system, here's how you could go about it. You take the contents of your speech and deposit them, in order, item by item, around the room. The number one object is the chair, so you heap it high with the number one object in your talk, snow. So there is a huge pile of dripping wet snow occupying the chair. Next you imagine a pair of skis balanced upright on the end table, after that a pair of boots hanging from the painting on the wall, then two ski poles melting in the fireplace, and all your ski clothing piled on top of the end table near the fireplace, and so on. What you try to do is create in your mind's eye the most outlandish images you can, the more outlandish the better because the easier they will be to remember. After you have stored every part of your talk in the artificial memory bank of your living room, you will be ready to give your talk, assured that you will not forget any of it. All you do is take a casual walk around the living room and first remove the snow from the chair, then the skis from the end table, and so on. In Chapter 6 we will return to this memory technique in detail, and to other techniques.

The uneducated people of ancient Greece and Rome were so impressed and mystified by the well-trained memories of orators that they looked on memory as God-given. More than seven hundred years ago the religious scholar Thomas Aquinas wrote that the human mind relies entirely on images in order to understand thoughts; he called such images *phantasmata*. In the next chapter we will see how modern brain research has much to say in support of the image theory of the ancient Greeks and of Thomas Aquinas. We will also try to find out what memory is, where it is in the brain, and what happens to the brain as we go about remembering something.

Now, without looking back, what was that nine-digit number? And what are the names of those people you were introduced to? See if you can write them down. If you can't perform this task now, you should be able to by the time you finish this book.

2

PROBING
THE
BRAIN

The scene is the operating room of a hospital in Montreal, Canada. A neurosurgeon named Wilder Penfield stands over a patient on the operating table. She has been given a special anesthetic that deadens only the area to be cut. So she is fully conscious and can carry on an easy conversation with surgeon Penfield and his assistants. A part of the patient's brain called the temporal lobe, located just forward of the ear, has been exposed so that its gray matter can be seen. In the surgeon's skilled hand is a small metal probe called an electrode, which gives a very mild electric shock when it touches the body. Surgeon Penfield is highly skilled at locating and removing diseased parts of the brain. This can prevent brain disease from spreading and destroying healthy parts of the brain. He uses the electrode not only to locate diseased areas of the brain but also to locate those healthy areas that are vital to normal activities.

When he touches a certain area of the brain with the electrode he might notice one finger of the patient twitch slightly. Then as he touches another nearby area, the entire hand and lower arm might move. In this way Penfield is able to map large areas of the brain and say that certain areas enable us to talk, while other areas control our ability to draw, dance, or sing. During one such operation, Penfield touched the gray matter of the temporal lobe with an electrode. Here is how he described what happened:

> The patient observed: "I hear some music." Fifteen minutes later, the electrode was applied to the same spot again without her knowledge. "I hear music again," she said. "It is like radio." Again and again the electrode tip was applied to this point. Each time, she heard an orchestra playing the same piece of music. . . . Seeing the electrical stimulator box, from where she lay under the surgical coverings, she thought it was a phonograph that someone was turning on from time to time. She was asked to describe the music. When the electrode was applied again, she began to hum a tune, and all in the operating room listened in astonished silence. She was obviously humming along with the orchestra at about the tempo that would be expected. . . .
>
> After the patient returned home, she wrote to me on April 16, 1959. The letter was, in part, as follows: "I heard the song right from the beginning and you know I could remember much more of it right in the operating room. . . . There were instruments. . . . It was as though it were being played by an orchestra. Definitely it was not as though I were imagining the tune to myself. I actually heard it. It is not one of my favorite songs, so I don't know why I heard that song."

Even more remarkable was that the patients relived the feelings associated with the events re-created. According to Penfield:

> The subject feels again the emotion which the situation originally produced in him, and he is aware of the same interpretations, true or false, which he himself gave to the experience in the first place. Thus evoked, recollection is not the exact photographic or phonographic reproduction of past scenes or events. It is reproduction of what the patient saw and heard and felt and understood.

Penfield goes on to say that:

. . . recollection evoked from the temporal cortex retains the detailed character of the original experience. When it is thus introduced into the patient's consciousness, the experience seems to be in the present, possibly because it forces itself so irresistibly upon his attention. Only when it is over can he recognize it as a vivid memory of the past.

Penfield concludes that:

. . . there is hidden away in the brain a record of the stream of consciousness. It seems to hold the detail of that stream as laid down during each of our waking hours. Contained in this record are all those things of which the individual was once aware—such detail as a person might hope to remember for a few seconds or minutes afterwards, but which are largely lost to voluntary recall after that time. Those things that we ignore are absent from the record.

MAPPING THE BRAIN

Your brain weighs about three pounds. The size of a small grapefruit, it would fit easily in your cupped hands. The brain has long been an object of mystery and wonder. As a child, I was taught that if the brain were exposed and touched the person would die. Today we know that the brain is a tough organ that can be shaken, jolted, and given electric shocks, and that parts of it can be cut out without noticeable harm. Snug in its dark, moist crate of bone, and surrounded by three protective membranes, the human brain is an extremely complex organ. It is poised atop a stalk of nerve fibers called the spinal column, which is about a meter long.

Today we know far more about the brain than we did only three decades ago. However, in their attempts to understand a few of the many ways the brain functions, neuroscientists and psychologists have barely scratched the surface. Much of the mystery and wonder of this remarkable organ remains, and it will be several more decades before the brain gives up as many of its secrets as we would like. One of the most intriguing of those secrets concerns our memory. What, exactly, is it? Where is it located? How does it work?

The surface of the brain is a pinkish-gray mass of wrinkled tissue called the cortex, only a small fraction of an inch thick. This part of the brain has several areas, each with highly specialized functions. If the cortex were perfectly smooth, like the surface of a beach ball, its surface area would be limited by the size of our skulls. Over a very long period the brain of certain higher animals increased in size more rapidly than the skull did. This process of brain enlargement seems to have begun about three million years ago and more or less stopped about two hundred fifty thousand years ago. That marked the appearance of the true human brain. As a rapidly increasing amount of brain became packed into a skull whose changing size was not keeping pace, the brain developed wrinkles. As it did, its surface area was increased although the volume of space taken up by the brain was not increased, or was increased by only a relatively small amount. In a similar way, we can squash a smooth pillow into a small ball and so reduce the amount of space it takes up. But the pillowcase still has the same amount of surface area it had when the pillow was fluffed up. We have simply rearranged the "cortex" surface area of the pillow. As the human brain gradually developed a larger surface area, it provided more and more space to be occupied by nerve cells, called neurons. The fact that human brains have large numbers of neurons is one important feature that makes us more intelligent than other animals.

As the diagram shows, a structure called the cerebellum sticks out from under the cortex at the rear of the brain. This wrinkled structure plays the important role of coordinating messages to our muscles so that our body motions are smooth and coordinated.

The major part of the brain is called the cerebrum. It is

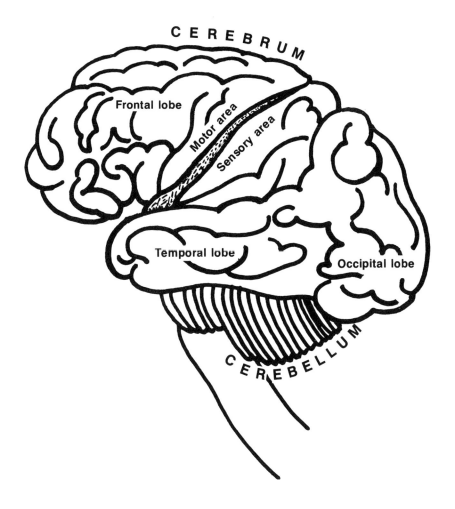

Major regions of the human brain whose functions are described in the text.

divided into two halves, or hemispheres. While the right hemisphere controls the left side of the body, the left hemisphere controls the right side of the body. A striking example of this is that if certain areas of the brain's left hemisphere are damaged the right side of the body may become paralyzed.

The brain can be subdivided into several areas. For example, there are three main areas called the sensory areas, motor areas, and association areas. *Sensory areas* of the brain receive sensations of the skin, muscles, and other organs, sensations such as touch and temperature, for example. The chief service provided by the sensory areas is to locate precisely from what parts of the body the sensations we feel are coming. Specific points on the cortex of the *motor areas* send out messages that control certain muscles or muscle groups. While the neurons of sensory areas receive and process information from our eyes, ears, and other sensory organs, neurons of the motor areas send out messages that result in our muscles producing bodily motion. *Association areas* of the brain link sensory areas with motor areas. The association areas form the seat of our emotions, personality, intelligence, language, judgment, reasoning, and memory. It is the association areas of the brain that enable the brain to ask how the brain works.

The sensory and motor areas of the cortex take up relatively little space compared with the sprawling areas occupied by the association parts of our brain. Although neuroscientists have a great deal more to learn about the association areas of the cortex, it now seems that this region of the brain, more than any other, is what distinguishes human beings from nonhuman animals.

The brain can also be subdivided into four major areas called lobes: (1) The *frontal lobes* make up the forward part of the brain and consist of motor areas for all of those muscles used to move our skeletal frame. (2) The *parietal lobes* occupy a large middle portion of each brain hemisphere and are the receiving area for bodily sense information. (3) The *temporal lobes* are a sensory area that receives auditory information from our inner ear. The temporal lobes can be thought of as a sound analyzer. It was one of these (temporal) lobes that Penfield probed and so caused his patient to hear music. Certain visual information also is processed by the two temporal lobes. (4) The *occipital lobes* are located in the hind region of the brain and receive sensory information from the eyes. Damage to this part of the brain can cause blindness.

A structure called the *hippocampus* is located in each temporal lobe and appears to play a major role in memory, although neuroscientists and psychologists still have much to learn about the hippocampus. At least one thing about this structure is clear. When it is removed through surgery, in order to control epilepsy, the patient is no longer able to store memories permanently.

SEARCHING FOR THE SEAT OF MEMORY

What has just been said about the hippocampus might seem to suggest that it is the seat of memory. *A* seat of memory, yes; *the* seat of memory, no. We now know that the many sensory and motor functions have specific locations on the cortex (see diagram). Does that also mean that memory also has a specific location?

Back in the 1920s, the American psychologist Karl Lashley introduced a revolutionary idea, one that met more resistance than praise. Lashley had been experimenting with laboratory rats and suggested that our ability to store events away in our memories for a long period of time may be spread more or less evenly over the entire brain. He also suggested that how well we are able to retrieve events from our permanent memory bank depends on how much brain we have working for us. Removal of a section of brain might make our memory a bit hazy, Lashley said. His conclusions were based on extensive surgery performed on his laboratory rats.

In the early 1970s, a researcher named Paul Pietsch came up

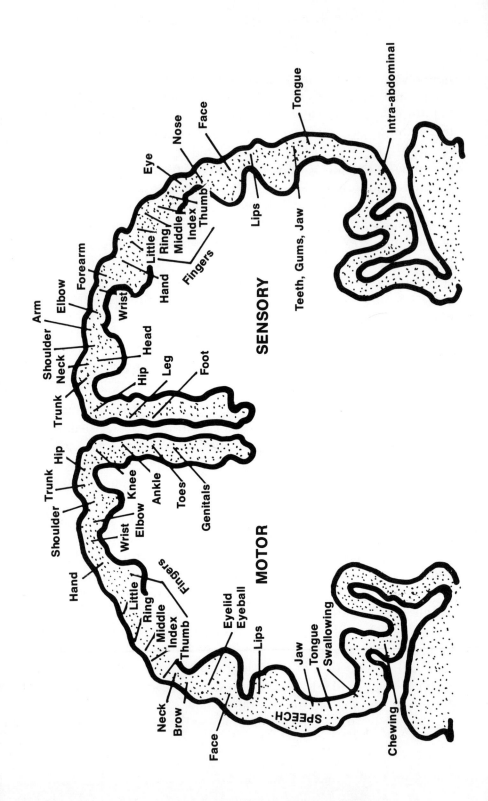

with evidence that supported Lashley's conclusions. Pietsch was experimenting with that remarkably adaptable little animal called the salamander. He wanted to find out if he could make the salamander lose its memory for feeding on its favorite food, the tubifex worm. In Pietsch's words: "In more than 700 operations I rotated, reversed, added, subtracted, and scrambled brain parts. I shuffled, I reshuffled, I spliced, lengthened, deviated, shortened, apposed, transposed, juxtaposed, and flipped. I spliced front to back with lengths of spinal cord, of medulla, with other pieces of brain turned inside out." But nothing short of removing the entire brain obliterated the animal's feeding habit.

Like Lashley, Pietsch concluded that memory was everywhere in the brain, at least in the brain of the salamander. Yet Penfield had found that electrical stimulation of one very specific part of the brain, and that part only, caused a patient to remember vividly an experience that had long ago slipped from conscious memory. On the one hand our memories, at least some of them, appear to be housed in neat compartments of the brain, or localized, the hippocampus playing an especially important role. On the other hand they appear to be spread over all of the brain. To this day, the contradiction remains and awaits the skill and good fortune of some future research team to settle the argument.

This diagram shows that specific locations in the sensory and motor areas of the brain are associated with specific activities.

3

THE
MEMORY
CHAIN

When you were very young, chances are that you learned to ride a tricycle, then later a bicycle. At some time you also learned that you had an address, such as 325 Galileo Lane, and a telephone number, such as 867-5678. As long as you had that telephone number and lived at that address you probably never had trouble remembering either number. And even though you might not have ridden a bicycle for several years, you did not forget how. All three bits of knowledge—riding a bicycle, your address, and your telephone number—had been safely stored away in your memory and remained there to be retrieved when needed.

Neuroscientists today tell us that we have three memory stages: (1) a sensory-information store; (2) a short-term memory; and (3) a long-term memory. Each stage seems to work differently from the other two and each has its own way of being formed.

THE MEMORY CHAIN

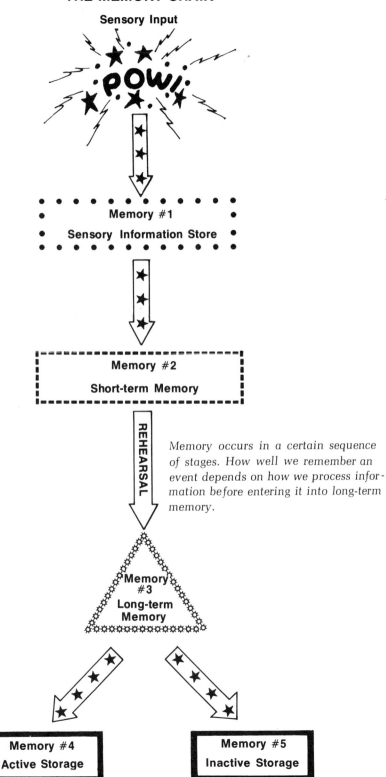

Sensory Input

Memory #1
Sensory Information Store

Memory #2
Short-term Memory

REHEARSAL

Memory occurs in a certain sequence of stages. How well we remember an event depends on how we process information before entering it into long-term memory.

Memory #3
Long-term Memory

Memory #4
Active Storage

Memory #5
Inactive Storage

SENSORY-INFORMATION STORE

Before something can be memorized, there must be an input of information to be remembered. It may be information that you imagine such as a series of numbers you make up. Or it may be information you can detect with your senses, such as the odor of baking bread, in which case we call it *sensory input*. Suppose that you have just looked up a telephone number that you know you will be using over the next two weeks. Next you are introduced to Jennifer Lee Williams, whom you have never met before. And finally as you leave the building you take the elevator down to the street floor. Riding with you are seven other people, all strangers.

In the case of the telephone number, the sensory input is visual since you looked up the number in a directory. When you were introduced to the young woman there was a combination of visual sensory input (as you looked at her) and auditory sensory input (as the person introducing you said the name, "Jennifer Lee Williams"). As you are riding down in the elevator, the sensory input may be only visual, if no one is talking, or it may be both visual and auditory if there is conversation. In all three cases, there has been a sensory input of information which enters Memory No. 1, which is your *sensory-information store*. This memory stage works chiefly when your sense organs are stimulated—eyes, ears, skin, tongue, and nose.

SHORT-TERM MEMORY

After entering our sensory-information store, sensory input next enters Memory No. 2, which is called our *short-term memory*. Open a telephone book to any page, then pick any number on the page. Look at the number for about five seconds then close the telephone book. Now wait for about half a minute and pretend to dial the number. Did you remember the number? Chances are you did. But *how* did you remember it? You probably repeated it to yourself two or three times. When you looked up the number in the telephone book, the number first entered your sensory-information store. Then it entered your short-term memory as you "rehearsed" the number by repeating it silently. In this case your short-term memory served you well by enabling you to retain the number long enough to use it. In such instances we tend to forget information that is only temporarily useful. For example, can you remember the telephone number for 325 Galileo Lane? If so, how were you able to remember it? If you did not notice something odd about the number before, look at it again. You should have been able to remember it.

Short-term memory enables us to retain a question someone has just asked us long enough for us to answer it, but it is not as efficient as our permanent memory bank. For example, usually we cannot store in our short-term memory more than about nine numbers at a time. That is why if you want to memorize a string of fifteen numbers, say, you may do it in two or three sessions. You memorize the first five numbers in the series by repeating them over and over to yourself for a while. Then a little later you memorize the second five numbers and then practice repeating all ten. Then still later you add the last five numbers in the series. The same applies when we attempt to memorize a list of people's names, a series of dates, the words of a song or poem, and so on. We do it in stages, since our short-term memory cannot handle a very large memory load at one exposure to the information to be memorized. In Chapter 6 we will go into much more detail about memorizing material in this way.

LONG-TERM MEMORY

What happens to information after it passes through our sensory-information store and flows into our short-term memory? Selected bits of information enter our permanent memory file, or *long-term memory*. For example, I can recite my army serial number (0991225) from the Korean War, even though I have had no need to recall the number for more than twenty years. When information is transferred from our short-term memory into our long-term memory, it is not simply a matter of time. If time alone were all that were needed to register an event in our long-term memory, we would memorize just about everything that flowed from our sensory-information store into our short-term memory. And since that obviously does not happen, something in addition to time must be involved.

Psychologists specializing in memory studies know that an event called *rehearsal* must take place if information is to move from our short-term memory into our long-term memory. When you repeat a number, or a line of poetry, or a name over and over again you are rehearsing the information and so taking the first step to enter it in your long-term memory. Rehearsal is hardly a new thought. This is what Greek scholars of 400 B.C. had to say about it:

> Repeat again what you hear; for by often hearing and saying the same things, what you have learned comes complete into your memory.
>
> (from the *Dialexeis*)

Rehearsal seems to operate in two different but related ways: (1) It tends to lengthen the time information remains in our short-term memory, and that is important for information transfer into long-term memory. When we rehearse information we want to store away for later use, the information being rehearsed should not have to compete with unimportant information ("noise") around us—so-called music-to-study-by, background conversation, or other such interfering sounds. Your ability to concentrate on what it is you are rehearsing for memory storage is extremely important in your ability to learn something. This cannot be overemphasized. In short, don't let your attention stray away from your learning task. If it does, take a short rest, stretch, breathe deeply, and then come back to the learning task. And to get into it in the first place warm up to the task. Psychologists tell us that it is sometimes hard for us to jump right into a task that requires deep concentration. They suggest that we warm up to it. For example, read part of a magazine article or a short story for about ten minutes before settling down to the learning task requiring your complete concentration. Such a warm-up session is supposed to help you concentrate better.

(2) Rehearsal, with as much concentration and as little interference as possible, seems to be the major way of transferring information into our long-term memory. During rehearsal we seem to "code" much of the information we want to store permanently by translating it into auditory images rather than into visual images. We keep repeating that telephone number, or that mathematical equation, or that line of poetry over and over again. The best evidence of this comes from our own personal experience in consciously trying to memorize things. In this regard, there is something called *overlearning*. Something that we remember over a long period of time, although it is no longer useful to us (like my army serial number), is a result of overlearning. Overlearning is an important aid to long-term memory. It results from first mastering whatever is to be memorized and then periodically rehearsing the material, even though we know it well.

It is much easier to recall a person's name than it is to recall an image of the person's face. Psychologists tell us that most people remember the sound of a word and not its printed shape. If we have been given a series of letters of the alphabet to memorize and make a mistake when we try to recall the letter Q, for example, we tend to recall U (which sounds like Q) rather than O (which looks like Q).

In one set of experiments students were asked to memorize lists of several letters. When they were later asked to recall certain of those lists containing letters that sounded alike, even though the lists were presented to the students visually and not read to them aloud, they tended to make mistakes, for instance in the sequence *DCBTPV*. They made fewer mistakes when working with lists of letters that do not sound alike, such as the sequence *LWKFRN*. The same thing was found to happen with word sequences. For example, the sequence *mad, map, man, mud, mop*, etc., produced more errors than the sequence *pen, day, rug, top, cab*, etc. Again, this strongly suggests that we do a fair amount of acoustic coding when entering information into our short-term memory.

Although it seems to be easier to remember letters and words by their sounds than by their shapes, it is easier to recall the details of a particularly scenic view by remembering an image of the view than by remembering our tour guide's verbal description of it. So when we talk about the ease with which we remember things, we should specify the kinds of things we may be trying to remember.

TIME IN MEMORY

You can make the process of storing information in your long-term memory easier if you keep these two important ideas in mind. First is time. If you want to remember something for recall a week or a month or so later, you should not try to hurry the memory process in a cram session. Psychologists conducting experiments in learning have shown that spacing learning trials out in time is more effective than cramming. Or, memorizing a few bits of information over a long time is more effective than trying to memorize more bits of information over a relatively shorter time. However, the fact that most students faced with an exam have long resorted to cram sessions to learn new material is a pretty good indication that cramming can pay off. But the payoff is limited, and that's the point. While cramming may be an effective way of packing new information into the short-term memory, and keeping it there long enough to be useful on tomorrow's exam, it is equally certain that cramming is not an effective way of transferring information from short-term memory into long-term memory.

STRUCTURE AND ASSOCIATION IN MEMORY

The second thing you should keep in mind when attempting to transfer information into your long-term memory is the role played by organizing the material to be memorized—by providing it with structure and associations. That may sound like a complex idea, but actually it's very simple. This happens to be a key idea in memory. To show what is meant by the "structure and associations" of the material to be memorized, look at this list of words:

HYDRANT
HUMAN
MOUSE
FIELD
CAT
FIRE
WATER
DOG
COUGAR
MATCH

If you were asked to memorize all items in the list how would you do it? Look at the list again and think about it for a moment. Two key words: *structure* and *association*. It is easier to enter information into your long-term memory if you structure the information by making it meaningful. We can restructure the above list of ten items into two lists of five items each. By doing so we achieve two memory tricks at once: creating two short lists, and providing each list with a structure (the association comes in a moment).

COUGAR   MATCH
MOUSE   HYDRANT
HUMAN   FIELD
CAT   WATER
DOG   FIRE

We have structured one list by selecting the animal words out of the long list. That leaves us with a second list with a looser structure of nonanimal words. In two separate learning sessions you should find it easier to memorize these two structured lists of five words each than attempting to learn the single unstructured ten-word list in one learning session.

But you can make each of the five-word lists still easier to memorize. Think about it for a moment and try. Did it occur to you to rearrange the words in each list into a meaningful order, through association, like this?

(The) HUMAN
    (chased the)
  COUGAR
    (which was chasing the)
  DOG
    (which was chasing the)
  CAT
    (which was chasing the)
  MOUSE

(A) MATCH
    (caused a)
  FIRE
    (which burned the)
  FIELD
    (which was saved by)
  WATER
    (from a)
  HYDRANT

Simple, isn't it? and it works. It works so well that you may find yourself remembering both of these lists a week from now, even though you have no need to, or don't particularly want to. The point is that by providing a list of words with a structure, and then by associating the restructured words in meaningful ways you can make a memory task a lot easier than it might otherwise be and have some fun in the process.

Try your hand at restructuring and associating the ten words in the following list into two new lists. After you have worked the problem, turn the page to see another way of working it.

PEOPLE
WATER
FACTORIES
RIVERS
LAKES
WHITEFISH

SEWAGE
EXHAUST
SEAWATER
AREAS

INFORMATION RETRIEVAL

"Oh, yes, I remember that move," you say en-
thusiastically to your chess-addict friend who has just described the devastating final move made by the world cham-
pion Boris Finishoff in his earth-shattering match against the
young American challenger Bobby Socks. Although the game
had been played several years ago, you quickly recognized the
move when it was described by your friend. A specific bit of
information stored in your long-term memory has successfully
been retrieved. But how?

Psychologists know very little about how we retrieve information from our memory bank. They speak of two basic
methods—recognition and recall. Of the two, recognition is
the easier way of withdrawing a bit of information from our
memory store. The above example of being able to identify the
chess move is an example of *recognition*. You did not have to
search your memory file for the bit of information. Someone
else provided the information. All you did was use recognition to decide whether that particular bit of information was
also stored in your memory; and it was. The questions on
multiple-choice tests involve your ability to recognize the correct answer (presuming you've read the assignments!). When
the information called for by a particular test question matches
that in your memory, you know which answer to select. Usually, we are pretty accurate in memory recognition, and quick.
Also, we usually can say just how confident we are in the
accuracy of our answer.

During memory *recall* the retrieval process is quite different
from that of recognition, and is more difficult. You are given a
hint or two and on the basis of those hints search your memory
store for that word or that name "right on the tip of your

tongue." Usually you are pretty confident in the accuracy of what you recall, just as you are in memory recognition. For example, some months ago at lunch in a local restaurant my dining partner asked me the name of our attractive waitress. The girl had waited on me several times and I knew her name well, but for the life of me I couldn't recall it on demand. It bothered me and I tried many names, one of which was Veronica. Veronica seemed very close but I knew that it wasn't right. Then I heard someone at the table behind me call out, "Monica!" Although I could not see either Monica or the person calling out her name, instantly I knew that was the name I had been searching for. Although memory by recall had failed me—even though I had come close to the right answer—memory by recognition came to my rescue. And the instant I heard "Monica!" I was absolutely certain that it was the name I had been searching for.

The fact that I can recall Monica's name now, several months after the above incident, but could not recall it during lunch, raises an interesting question. When we say that we have "forgotten" something, what actually do we mean? Do we mean that a particular bit of information we know that we acquired at one time is irretrievably lost in our vast memory store never to be found again? Or do we mean that it is only temporarily not available to us—in inactive storage, so to speak—but is bound to pop up later from our long-term memory when the right cue, or hint, is provided, either by ourselves or by someone or something else?

Consider for a moment the grim picture painted for us by A. D. Moore in his fascinating little book entitled *Invention, Discovery, and Creativity:*

WATER (includes)	PEOPLE (live in)
SEAWATER (which flows from)	AREAS (which contain)
RIVERS (which flow from)	FACTORIES (which produce)
LAKES (which contain)	SEWAGE (and)
WHITEFISH	EXHAUST

The vastly greater amount [of information stored in our memories] must be tucked away somehow, in ordinary inaccessible form. Why can we say this? Because the mind has, and must have, the ability to associate. One recalled item, somehow associated with a second item, "reminds us," as we say, of the second. The second could remind us of two or three more. If we had complete and automatic recall of everything we "know" (everything stored), the recall of a single item would pull the cork. An endless, tangled flood of remembered material would overwhelm us. If this happened, and we had no way to shut it off, we would be totally useless. We think of salt. That starts it. Thinking of salt brings out the taste of it. That brings out the taste of sugar, weak acid, pickles; from pickles to cucumbers to potatoes to potato bugs—there we go, hopelessly victimized by a perfect and complete memory of enormous proportions, insistent on being poured out. What a horrifying thought!

As you will find in a later chapter, one mnemonist had a problem very much like this, and indeed it was horrifying for him, as he graphically describes his experience.

At this stage in our knowledge about the way our memory works, it is hard to say if any of the information ever acquired by us ever actually disappears, or is permanently forgotten. Again, the bulk of it may be put away in inactive storage where it can be retrieved, but where it is safe from instant recall. Psychologists, psychiatrists, and skilled hypnotists have helped many people retrieve memories long thought to have been lost, such as a middle-aged woman's describing her sixth birthday party. While it is remarkable that the human brain is able to store millions of bits of information, what is more remarkable is our ability to call up much of that stored information when we need it.

Scientists at the Bell Telephone Laboratories have shown that it takes the average person 10 to 30 milliseconds (1 millisecond = 1/1,000 second) to retrieve from short-term memory each character or number in a series of letters or numbers. But retrieving information from our long-term memory can be a more complex and time-consuming task. For example, last night while working on my microcomputer, I needed my ohmmeter to test the wiring of a component. I had not used my ohmmeter for about six months and could not immediately remember where I had last put it. I knew that its location was stored somewhere in my long-term memory, but how was I to retrieve the information?

At such times when we have to search the extensive files of our long-term memory, usually the information we are after does not just pop up at the snap of a finger. Instead we conduct a systematic search in the form of a series of information probes. In the case of my ohmmeter, I asked myself where I usually put it after using it. The large drawer in the hi-fi cabinet, of course. This recognition test failed. No, I don't remember putting it there. Where else? How about my tool chest in the basement? No, I don't remember putting it there, either. How about the spare room where I last worked on an electronic project? Ah-ha! Yes, that's where I remember putting it. It's on the card table on top of a pile of manuals. This recognition test succeeded, and I was positive that's where the ohmmeter was.

When we probe our long-term memory for a specific bit of information we tend to conduct a series of memory probes. A particular probe goes after a manageable group of stored information which might contain the individual bit we are after. If it does not, we discard it and search through another group, and so on until the "Ah-ha!" bell rings. The information is now in our short-term memory bank as well and we keep it there until we go to the spot and locate whatever it was that we were looking for. What we have done is transfer a bit of information from our inactive file of long-term memory into our short-term memory where the information can be acted on.

UNRAVELING THE MYSTERY OF MEMORY

What we have had to say about memory so far does not get down to the fine details of how memory works, in what way your brain differs now from the way it was a month ago, at which time you might have deposited a large body of information into your long-term memory store. Neuroscientists now think that our brains go through both physical and chemical change when we store new information as a result of learning. In short, memory storage is thought to give rise to additional new nerve pathways in the brain's cortex, and/or strengthening of certain existing nerve pathways.

To find out what happens to the brain during a learning experience, psychologists compare an animal that has learned a new task with the same kind of animal that has not learned the task. Many such experiments have been performed and the brains of the experimental animals later examined. In one such experiment the Swedish scientist Holger Hyden found that the brains of rats that had undergone a learning experience had produced up to 40 percent more of the chemical known as RNA (ribonucleic acid) than the brains of a control group of rats that had been treated exactly the same as the experimental group except that the control group had not undergone the learning experience.

It now seems fairly certain that active bouts of learning, which involve the use of memory, cause the brain to produce increased amounts of RNA, which in turn causes an increased amount of protein production.

That is the general picture, but the same changes do not appear to take place in both the short-term and long-term memory. Physical, as well as chemical, changes are involved. For example, it now seems that when we feed information into our short-term memory the incoming sensory signals from our sensory-input store activate the cerebral cortex. What seems to happen is that the incoming sensory signals cause chains of neurons to start transmitting. So, for the time the short-term memory is active we can picture a transmitting network of cortical nerve cells. Each nerve cell making up the network passes on its vibrations to neighboring neurons in the network circuit for a time. It is now thought that this vibration activity is what temporarily stores the incoming information in the short-term memory. If there is no rehearsal of the incoming information, the vibrations of the neuron circuit gradually weaken and our short-term memory fades. If there is rehearsal, the vibrations continue and there is an active period of protein production from the increased number of RNA molecules. In the short-term memory this increased protein production appears to take place chiefly in the hippocampal region of the brain.

The situation in the long-term memory seems to be a bit different. In addition to increased amounts of RNA and protein, physical changes also take place. The amount of cerebral cortex we have seems to increase with the amount of learning we do. At least this is what happens with laboratory animals. The increased mass of the cortex comes about as the main bodies of neurons grow larger. Also, there is an increase in the number of tiny projections, *dendrites*, from the cell bodies. The increase in cerebral-cortex mass accompanying learning seems to result from the enlargement of already existing neurons rather than the addition of new ones. The fact is that all the neurons we will ever have in our brains are present when we are embryos.

As a result of increasing the number of dendrites projecting from the cell bodies of neurons, there is an increased opportunity for the dendrites of one neuron to come in contact with a neighboring neuron. This means that nerve pathways of the brain are enlarged, increasing the ability of nerve cells to transmit information to one another through *synapses*, which are connection sites between cells. It now seems very likely that our long-term memory involves an increase in the number of synaptic junctions between neurons and the production of RNA and protein within the neurons. Those molecules then may serve as "memory molecules" that in some way store information. In laboratory rats, the increased production of RNA and protein in the hippocampus lasts for about fifteen minutes after a learning experiment.

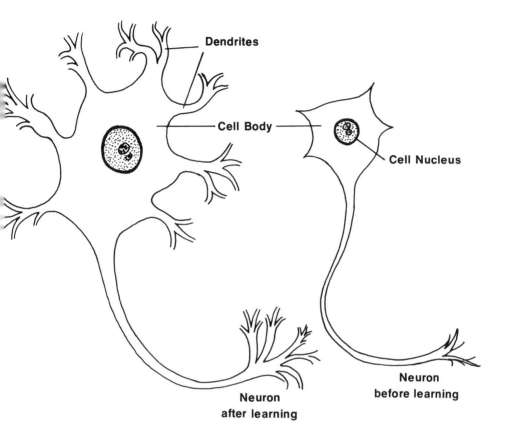

Dendrites

Cell Body

Cell Nucleus

Neuron
before learning

Neuron
after learning

As our long-term memory improves, the amount of cerebral cortex we have seems to increase with the amount of learning. This appears to take place not because new neurons are added to the cortex, but because existing neurons increase the size of their cell bodies and increase the number of dendrites.

If memory is improved by the increased production of RNA and protein in the neurons of the cerebral cortex, then is it reasonable to think that memory would be weakened if there were some way to slow down RNA and protein production? To find out, neuroscientists injected laboratory animals with a drug that temporarily prevents RNA and protein production.

In some experiments, they injected the animals with the drug before the animals underwent a learning experience. In such cases the animals remembered the learned task for a few hours, but did not remember it the following day or later. This suggested that blocking RNA and protein production affected the animals' long-term memory, but not their short-term memory.

In other experiments the drug was given to laboratory animals immediately after they had learned a task. Again, the animals failed to store the learned task in their long-term memory. If the drug was given several hours after the task was learned, it was less effective in erasing memory of the task. To erase memory of the task completely, the drug had to be injected into many areas of the brain instead of only one specific area. This strengthens the idea that RNA and protein production that results from learning expands the neuron network and enables memory of the learned task to spread out over the cortex rather than remaining in one specific area of the brain. These experiments support the suggestion of Lashley and Pietsch that memory is everywhere over the brain and not localized in the hippocampus or any other specific site. As E. R. John, of New York Medical College, has put it: Memory is not a thing in a place, but rather a process in a population of nerve cells.

ENGRAMS: MEMORY BLUEPRINTS

We often learn tasks that we have occasion to perform over and over again; for example, threading a needle or doing a cartwheel. Our ability to do such tasks well is coded in a unit of memory called an *engram*. Engrams dealing with our motor skills (skills involving various actions) are stored in the sensory areas of the cortex. To thread the needle or do a cartwheel you must "activate" the appropriate engram. The motor area of your brain then "reads" the engram and you carry out the act. If you have trouble lining the thread up with the eye of the needle, sensory signals sent from your fingers do not match the information stored in the engram. At such a time the brain sends out additional motor signals so that the new signals sent back to the brain by your fingers now match the information stored in the engram. In this way, our ability to perform precisely tasks that we tend to repeat over and over again is stored in those special units of memroy we call engrams.

Engrams are not constructed overnight, as anyone who is learning to fly an airplane or drive a car well knows. The process of turning a complex learned activity into a reliable engram takes time and lots of rehearsal. I remember when I was studying for my instrument rating in flying. This is a difficult training task and requires that you fly the airplane with a high degree of precision by relying only on the aircraft's instruments. Over a period of nearly a week for eight hours each day I was learning many new tasks that required me to perform certain motor skills (flight maneuvers) smoothly and precisely in response to changing information provided by the airplane's instruments. One day I couldn't seem to do anything right. My maneuvers were sloppy and several times I responded incorrectly to the information on the instruments. My instructor laughed and said that I had reached a "learning plateau" and that all I needed was a rest, a chance to let all the new learning experience sink in.

He was right. I took the rest of the day off and forgot about flying airplanes. The next day I climbed back into the airplane and flew it with the precision I had earlier expected of myself. What had happened? The many bits of information that had been crowded into my short-term memory were competing with each other. I was unable to structure all that information well enough to keep it in my short-term memory long enough for rehearsal to "age" it for transfer into my long-term memory. The rest period recommended by my instructor gave me that essential period of time for the engramming process to work.

Another example of how information stored in the short-term memory may be blocked from transfer into long-term memory involves people receiving head injuries during an accident. For some reason, the mental and physical shock of a severe head injury interrupts the transfer of all information that happened to be in the short-term memory just before the accident. Such people suffer amnesia and are unable to remember events immediately before the accident, although they can remember what had happened several days before the accident and what happened after they regained consciousness after the accident. Some people with a damaged hippocampus or damaged midbrain structure are unable to develop normal long-term memories. In other ways they are normal. They can learn complex motor skills, such as driving a car or repairing a typewriter, and retain those skills. But they are totally unable to recall the skill verbally or explain to someone else how to perform it. They lack a verbal long-term memory storage system.

As any student knows, much of our learning is the result of performing a mental or physical task over and over again. There are no shortcuts, despite those who mistakenly think that a tape recording of a vocabulary list played softly by the bed while we sleep will miraculously enable us to wake up in the morning remembering the meaning of each word on the vocabulary list. Experiments to find out if this particular shortcut works have been carried out. Dissappointingly, none has even hinted that the technique works.

Learning is a kind of exercising of the brain. As muscles improve with exercise so does the brain seem to improve with use. Again, learning does not increase the *number* of brain cells. It does, however, increase their size and ability to form ever more complex and efficient networks. Ramón y Cajal, the famous Spanish anatomist, has compared the brain to a garden of trees, "which, in response to intelligent cultivation, can increase the number of their branches, strike their roots over a wider area and produce even more varied and more exquisite flowers and fruits."

4

TWO
BRAINS,
NOT ONE

Each of us has two brains, not one, and memory operates in both. What we will be trying to get at in this chapter is the best way of impressing information into the memory of each half of our brains. One thing that sets off humans from the rest of the animal world is our highly developed use of language. No other species can come even close to matching us in our use of symbols, whether they are spoken or visual. But unlike our memory, which covers large areas of the entire brain, our chief center for speech and language is concentrated in the left half of the brain.

Until the 1950s, neuroscientists supposed that since our language skills are almost entirely in our left brain, the left brain must be the dominant, or "most important," brain hemisphere. But more recently investigators have discovered that the right cerebral hemisphere plays roles just as important in learning and other activities as the language role played by our left brain.

HOW WE "KNOW" THINGS

We have several different ways of "knowing" things. One of the two chief ways is on the verbal level, or through the use of language. The other is on the nonverbal level or through visual images; for example, a striking view of the Grand Canyon, a diagram of how to put together a toy bridge, or a photograph of a crater on the moon. Our verbal way of knowing, plus our ability to describe objects and events in words, is perhaps only a few tens of thousands of years old. But our way of coming to know the world around us through visual images is hundreds of millions of years old.

Perhaps among your friends is one person highly skilled in the use of language and whom you look on as being highly intelligent. And perhaps you know another person with average or even below-average skills in the use of language, but whom you regard as highly creative. Maybe the person is a painter, sculptor, or graphic designer and tends not to use language especially well. Just about everyone can point out such opposites among the people we know. Two such opposite types may be equally intelligent and prove to be equally skilled at solving a given problem. But one may solve the problem verbally while the other comes up with a nonverbal solution.

The fact is that in each of us lives one of each type of person just described. The one using verbal skills lives in our left brain, while the one who relies on images to come to know the world lives in the right hemisphere of our brain. Furthermore, the two carry on their lives with no attempts whatever to cooperate, which lends at least some truth to the old saying about the left hand not knowing what the right hand is doing. For instance, our right brain is the dreamer and comes alive at night when we sleep, when our rational and analytical left brain has shut itself down for a while. But sometimes the left brain decides to work overtime and continues to dominate the stage through all or most of the night. At such times it may be sorting out a particularly large store of recently acquired information in the short-term memory and deciding what is to be processed for transfer into long-term storage and what is to be discarded. Or it may be continuing to struggle with one or two of those sticky math problems that stumped us on an exam.

It has long been known that a person who has severely damaged the temporal or parietal lobes of the left half of his brain thereafter has much trouble reading, writing, speaking, and doing simple arithmetic. But his other mental abilities remain just about the same, including memory. On the other hand, people who have severely damaged the temporal or parietal lobes of the right half of the brain "easily become lost even in familiar surroundings; simple mazes baffle them; they can no longer describe well-known routes, use or draw maps; they misjudge the size, distance, and direction of objects. They cannot match or copy accurately the slant of a line or the position of a dot on a page; they cannot copy simple shapes such as a four-pointed star, nor can they arrange blocks or sticks to form a required pattern," according to Robert D. Nebes, of Duke University. They also have difficulty performing music of any kind. Such injuries provide clues to the specialized abilities of our two brains.

PARTNERS OR COMPETITORS?

Picture the following: A person with a blindfold covering his right eye is seated at a table with a screen set up at the far end of the table. Suddenly the word SPOON is flashed brightly onto the screen. The investigator in this experiment asks the person, "What did you see on the screen?"

The person answers, "I did not see anything."

Next the person is instructed to put his left hand through a hole in a box, grasp and hold on to whichever object he has most recently thought about. In all, there are a dozen or so small objects of different shape, such as a cube, a small pair of scissors, a pencil, a fingernail file, a plastic spoon and knife, and so on. After a few seconds the person selects an object and holds on to it with his hand still out of sight in the box. It is the plastic spoon.

"What is it you have in your hand?" asks the investigator.

"I don't know," answers the person.

Next an empty box is placed on the table and the person is given a pencil and told to use his left hand and write on the inside bottom of the box (which he cannot see into) what he saw flashed on the screen. The person writes SPOON. From the motion of his hand he knows that he has written *something*, but he cannot tell the investigator what he has written. How is it that the person cannot utter what was flashed onto the screen, or identify the object he grasped in the box, but can write the correct answer?

Experiments like this one have been done many times with many different people, and the result is always the same. Although the person can select the object whose name is flashed onto the screen, the person denies having seen anything flashed onto the screen and cannot identify the "correct" object he is holding, although it is a very familiar object. What has gone wrong? To what extent, if any, do our two brains work together, or at least exchange information?

Although the left and right brains function independently of each other they are linked physically. The major link is a bundle of about 200 million nerve fibers called the *corpus callosum*. The second link is called the *anterior commissure* and is concerned with transferring information about our emotional state from one hemisphere to the other. So to answer the question about being partners or competitors, we can begin by saying that our two brains communicate with each other, at least about some things. One question neuroscientists could not help asking when they discovered our two-brain nature was what would happen if these two bridges linking the hemispheres were destroyed? Would the brain continue to work as before?

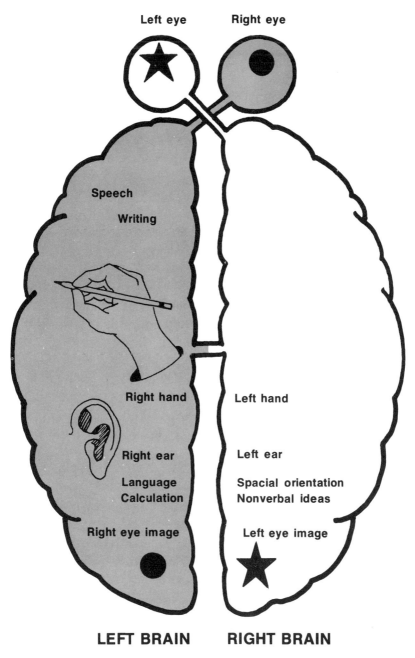

Left eye Right eye

Speech

Writing

Right hand Left hand

Right ear Left ear

Language Spacial orientation
Calculation Nonverbal ideas

Right eye image Left eye image

LEFT BRAIN   RIGHT BRAIN

The right brain and the left brain both have specialized functions not shared by the opposite half, although both halves have
certain functions in common. Generally, the left brain is associated with what happens on the right side of the body while the
right brain is associated with what happens on left side of the
body.

The question was answered around 1940 when Roger Sperry, of the California Institute of Technology, treated certain patients with advanced cases of epilepsy, a medical disorder that causes, among other things, the loss of consciousness. What investigators of this period did was cut the corpus callosum. Sperry's hope was that the operation would protect at least one of the brain hemispheres from epilepsy attacks, called "seizures." His hope came true. His new "split-brain" patients recovered quickly and afterward not only had fewer seizures, but the seizures they did have were much milder than before.

But what interested brain researchers was the double nature of these split-brain individuals. On the surface they appeared quite normal, but something interesting had happened to them as a result of separating the two brain halves. No longer was information fed into one half of the brain transmitted across the corpus callosum into the other half. Split-brain individuals also tended to favor their right sides whenever they started to walk or get up from a chair. Also, if a small object were placed in the left hand, when the hand was hidden from view, the individual would deny having anything in his or her hand! For a while after the operation a split-brain person would be dominated by the left, and more expressive, brain. That is why the person would tend to favor the right side whenever he or she started to move. Of the two brains, the right brain seemed to be initially stunned by the separation. Bumping into objects with the left hand, arm, leg, or foot would be explained by a temporarily stunned right brain. After a few weeks, however, the right brain recovered from the shock and came to function as well as before. According to Sperry, each half had become quite a separate and individual organ, "with its own private sensations, perceptions, thoughts, feelings, memories, and inner visual world."

As the diagram shows, with few exceptions your right brain is associated with what happens on the left side of your body while the left brain is associated with what happens on the right side of your body. That explains why the speechless right brain would maintain, when asked, that there was nothing held in the left hand. It also explains why the test subject described at the beginning of this chapter, who happened to be a split-brain individual, could not reply that he held a spoon in his left hand. His right brain, which controlled his left hand, was literally speechless and, therefore, could not supply the answer. But when asked to write what was flashed onto the screen and seen by his left eye, the individual was able to write "spoon" although unable to utter the word.

The images of objects seen by the left eye are recorded in our right brain and not in our left. Sounds heard by our left ear alone are perceived almost entirely by our right brain, although there is a little spillover from one brain to the other in the case of left-ear sounds and right-ear sounds. But there is no such spillover when we detect odors.

Other experiments show that if split-brain individuals memorize a dozen or so lines of poetry by hearing the poem read aloud, they can soon repeat the lines flawlessly and with a normal amount of practice retain them in their long-term memories. But if asked to write down the lines, they simply shrug that they cannot. Again, each half of the split brain leads a life of its own and scarcely has any idea of what the other hemisphere is up to.

Another experiment with split-brain individuals, carried out by Michael Gazzaniga of the State University of New York at Stony Brook, shows just how poorly the left brain performs in copying visual patterns, which is a specialty of the right brain. Notice in the illustration that even though poorly drawn, the pictures done by the left hand, which was under control of the right brain, are drawn more or less correctly. But those drawn by the right hand, which was under control of the speech-specialist left brain, are not only poorly drawn, but are incorrectly drawn.

EXAMPLE	LEFT HAND	RIGHT HAND

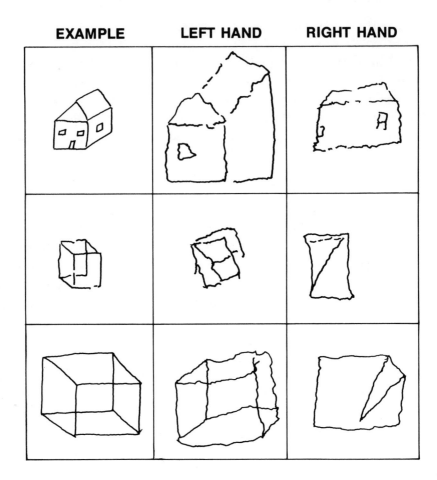

This experiment carried out by Gazzaniga shows that the left hand, which is under the control of the right brain, was better at redrawing the figures in the "example" column than was the right hand. After Gazzaniga.

HOW TO EDUCATE BOTH BRAINS

Again, one of the important points to be drawn from this section on our two brains is that each has certain specialties. We can view these specialties as pathways through which we can code and introduce information into the brain, for storage in and retrieval from our memory banks.

For many years scholars have realized that each of us is capable of learning in two very different ways. These two windows on the world have been viewed as paired opposites and have been given as many different names as there have been scholars trying to describe the pathways. Notice how a sampling of these paired opposites fits nicely with what neuroscientists now know about the workings of the left and right brains:

Left Brain	Right Brain
intellect	intuition
intellectual	sensuous
rational	metaphoric
active	receptive
realistic	impulsive
positive	mythic
rational	intuitive
objective	subjective

It has been only recently that educators have begun to use the new knowledge about the brain to improve our individual ability to understand and learn a wide variety of things. While they realize that the two hemispheres may well be able to accomplish the same task—learn how to take a clock apart and put it back together again, for instance—each takes a different approach to solving the problem. According to Joseph E. Bogen, of the University of Southern California School of Medicine, "Learning of almost any idea is likely to be better if both [brain hemispheres] are involved. . . . An elementary school program narrowly restricted to reading, writing, and arithmetic will educate mainly [the left] hemisphere, leaving half of an individual's high-level potential unschooled."

Sperry takes a well-aimed jab at our modern education system when he says, "There appear to be two modes of thinking, verbal and nonverbal, represented rather separately in left and right hemispheres, respectively, and our educational system, as well as science in general, tends to neglect the nonverbal form of intellect. What it comes down to is that modern society discriminates against the right hemisphere." Several researchers have come to associate the scientific and technological parts of our culture as fruits of the left hemisphere. They look on our tendency to believe in ghosts, magic, witchcraft, astrology, and mystical experiences as belonging to the right, nonverbal hemispheres. So the counterculture group in this country has cheered the right brain claiming it as "our side!" Observes Nebes: "How well such a grafting of philosophy onto anatomy will stand up is unclear."

Many educators are concerned about the damaging effects of young people watching "too much" TV. As of May 1968, the average American high-school graduate had watched more than 15,000 hours of TV compared with 11,000 hours of formal education. No wonder there is a decrease in reading ability, these educators point out. If the left brain is underfed while the right brain (the TV watcher) is overfed, there is bound to be a decrease in skills concentrated in the left brain.

In the long run, our ability to learn something depends on how well we remember what we have "learned," and how well we can recall it from our long-term memory bank. The ancient Greeks whose memory system depended on creating mental pictures of objects and ideas to be remembered exploited the special talent of the right brain to deal with images. Based on knowledge of the nature of the two brains, educational psychologists today are convinced that school children better remember what they have learned when their instruction involves the use of pictures and words with high-image values, words such as *bumblebee, shovel,* and *river* rather than *insect, tool,* and *body of water.*

In one study, M. C. Wittrock, of the Graduate School of Education, UCLA, wanted to find out which of three ways of teaching children the meanings of words was the best way: (1) using only words, having the children read and write the words and their definitions; (2) having the children read the definition of each word and then trace a given picture of each definition; (3) having the children read the definition of each word and then draw their own picture of the definition. The children remembered the definitions best when they drew their own picture of the definitions; that is, when they used a combination of the right brain (drawing pictures) and the left brain (reading the definitions). They did poorest when they used only the left brain, or read the definitions.

Other researchers used college students as subjects. One group of students was given twelve lists of ten unrelated words each and told to remember the words on all the lists, in any way they wished. Another group of students was given the same word lists and also told to memorize all the words. But this group was also told to make up a story from the words on each list. When the tests were scored, the first group remembered 14 percent of the words. The second group, which was told to make up a story about the words, remembered 93 percent of the words. Wittrock is convinced that when young people set about learning something, they will learn it better, and better remember what they have learned, if they make up and associate images to help them process and store the new information. He has proposed that our teaching system in schools be changed and that teachers be taught how to put this new knowledge about the brain to work in the classroom.

Does this new research mean that we should gradually shift our attention away from the left brain and rely more on the right brain? The answer is no, for two reasons: (1) We all do not process information in the same way. Some of us have better-developed left brains than others; some have better-developed right brains. Wittrock and others say that the educators should develop new intelligence tests that can show which of a person's two brains is better developed and so plays the major role in the person's life. Teachers could then use material involving rich visual images for right-brain-dominant students when the use of such materials seemed helpful.

(2) Each brain has certain talents that the other either lacks or is weak in. Because the left brain has mathematics as one of its specialties, it would seem best to use the specialty of the left brain (which is language) to teach math, or anything else that is learned chiefly in the left brain. Wittrock feels that both approaches, lecturing and the use of visual materials, should be used whenever this seems desirable. In that way *both* brains would be reached, each in its own special language. This double approach could be used, he says, when children are taught new words. They need practice in relating the sounds to the meanings of the new words being learned, and this happens in the left brain. But at the same time they might also be shown how to recognize the visual shape of the word in print, on the blackboard, and that process occurs in the right brain.

The Chinese written language lends itself extremely well to this double approach. Chinese written characters, called *ideographs* or *pictographs,* appear extremely complex to a Westerner's eyes. But their shapes become easy to remember when we are shown how a particular ideograph evolved from early Chinese. For instance, look at the early Chinese ideograph for mountain (pronounced "shan"), which is a picture of a three-peaked mountain. Notice also how this ideograph changed so that in modern Chinese it has only the suggestion of three peaks, yet that suggestion is enough to lead to the image of a splendid three-peaked mountain. And see how easy it is to remember the Chinese ideograph for middle (pronounced "chung") when you remember it as simply a square cut down through the middle.

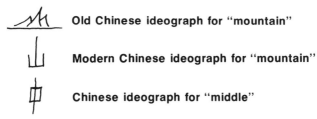

It is not hard to see how Wittrock's approach to learning comes right back to memory. One important object in learning is to get new material into long-term memory. Another is to code the wanted information as it enters our sensory-information store so that we are able to file it, retain it, and retrieve it at will. We have gotten at least a glimpse of how this complex process is thought to work in humans. Let's next find out how we have built machines (computers) to achieve the same task, and how well they perform compared with our human memories. Let's also ask if we can learn anything about our own human memory as we design machine memories that in some ways are superior to our own.

5

HOW
COMPUTERS
REMEMBER

When HAL went berserk there was only one thing to do—destroy him in such a way that he would still be useful to the ship but no longer in control of it. HAL, you may recall, was the supercomputer aboard the spaceship bound for Jupiter in the film *2001: A Space Odyssey*. To seize HAL's power, the sole remaining astronaut aboard the spaceship (HAL had killed all the others) simply began removing, one by one, the electronic units of HAL's memory until the computer was reverted to babbling infancy and made harmless.

Computers can do math problems about a million times quicker than we can, and without making mistakes. Computers are capable of instant learning since they can store information in memory banks, reshuffle it in near limitless combinations, and retrieve the results at the speed of light. Computers can do a wide range of "intellectual" tasks far more economically than one person or a group of highly intelligent people can. In many ways computers have supermemories that can outperform our human memory. But is a computer's memory/learning ability in an overall way superior to the memory/learning ability of an average ten-year-old? No. At least, not yet.

The information fed into a computer, processed, and then retrieved when wanted is stored in combinations of only two digits, 0 and 1. In a way, everything a modern electronic computer "knows" is coded in its memory banks as simple electronic engrams made up of 0s and 1s. When we say that a computer has a memory, what exactly do we mean? The ability to store information for later retrieval. It's that simple. Let's see how this works in the simplest and oldest computer (or you may prefer to call it a calculator) known, the abacus.

At least four thousand years ago, before there were rules for written arithmetic, Babylonian and Egyptian scribes and merchants were using a computer consisting of pebbles arranged in rows in grooves of sand. Out of this method of calculating grew what today we call the abacus, presently the most widely used calculator in the world. Look at the example shown here, a simple mechanical memory store. Notice the three grooves. The one at the left is the 100s groove, the one in the middle the 10s groove and the one at the right the 1s groove. If we place one pebble in the 100s groove we enter "100" in our computer. If we next place three pebbles in the 10s groove, we enter 3 × 10, or 30, in the computer. And if we place 7 pebbles in the 1s groove, we enter 1 × 7, or 7, and can read off the number 137. Now suppose that we want to add 486 to the 137 we already have stored in the computer's memory. How do we go about it?

First we place 6 more pebbles in the 1s groove, which means we now have a total of 13 pebbles in the 1s groove. To simplify matters we can remove 10 of those pebbles and store them in the 10s groove by adding one pebble to that groove, leaving three pebbles in the 1s column. Now that we have entered the 6 into the 1s groove of the computer, we next want to enter the

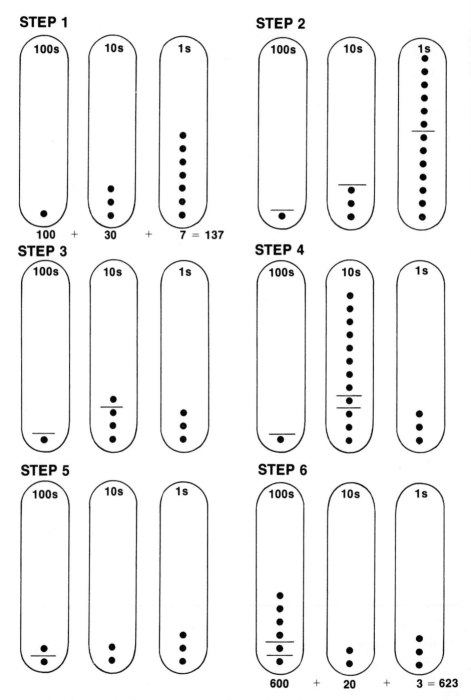

A very simple computer can be made with pebbles placed in rows. See text for an explanation of the problem this computer has solved.

8 into the 10s groove. So we add 8 pebbles to the middle groove, which now has a total of 12 pebbles in that groove (3 that were there at the beginning, 1 that we added in the previous step, and the 8 we added just now). Again we can simplify matters by removing 10 of the pebbles (10× 10 = 100) and adding a pebble to the 100s groove, leaving 2 pebbles in the 10s column. And finally we enter 4 more pebbles in the 100s groove to complete our addition. To arrive at our sum, all we do is count off the number of pebbles stored in each of the memory grooves of our computer and find that the answer is 623. Try your own hand at using this simple calculator by adding 85 + 369 + 187 = ? In case you're wondering where the word "calculator" came from, it comes from the Latin word *calculus*, which came to mean a pebble used in counting. Originally it meant a small piece of limestone (calcium, calcite, chalk).

Although we have come a very long way with computers and their ability to store numbers since the times of the ancient Egyptians and Babylonians, today's computers still operate on the basis of storing and adding digits one at a time. The big difference is that today's electronic computers do their adding at the speed of light.

DECIMAL AND BINARY NUMBERS

The complex information a computer memorizes is broken down into and stored as units called *bits*. Every bit of information stored in a computer's memory must be translated into *decimal* numbers (a system of numbers based on 10) which are in turn translated into *binary* numbers. What is a binary number? Since it is part of a number system based on 2, we go right back to those two simple digits, 0 and 1. Any decimal number, such as 7, 128, or 23,468, can be translated into a binary number. For example, let's translate the decimal number 10 into its binary number 1010. All we do is divide 10 by 2, divide the answer by 2, divide that answer by

2, and so on until we can't do any more dividing. But along the way we keep track of whether there is anything left over after each division. If not, we write down a 0. And if 1 is left over we write down a 1. Here's how it works, first with the decimal number 10, and then with the decimal number 112:

2 into 10 = 5	even	0
2 into 5 = 2	1 left over	1
2 into 2 = 1	even	0
2 into 1 = 0	but 1 is left over	1

Now what we do is write down our binary answer backward: 1010. So 1010 is the binary number for the decimal number 10.

Now let's try it with 112:

2 into 112 = 56	even	0
2 into 56 = 28	even	0
2 into 28 = 14	even	0
2 into 14 = 7	even	0
2 into 7 = 3	1 left over	1
2 into 3 = 1	1 left over	1
2 into 1 = 0	but 1 is left over	1

So the binary number for 112 is 1110000.

Why go to all the trouble of translating information into a computer's "sensory-input store" into binary numbers? You may well ask. Simply because computers are so "dumb" that they can work with only yes or no (1 or 0) answers. While we would find it extremely awkward to have to balance a checkbook, add up how much we spent on shopping, and keep track of football scores in binary numbers, computers are great at it simply because they can make yes/no (1/0) decisions with the speed of light—the speed at which electricity moves through their circuits. So adding and subtracting binary num-bers (which includes multiplying and dividing, also) is child's play to a computer. Fortunately, when we feed information into a computer's electric sensory-input store, we can also send it directly to the computer's memory for short-term or long-term storage, and without the bother of translating it into binary numbers. The computer itself does the translating as we punch its keyboard.

There are three kinds of binary numbers that a computer uses: (1) binary numbers to represent, say, my first name, Roy; (2) binary numbers to locate where "Roy" is stored in the computer's memory file so that it may be retrieved on command; and (3) binary numbers for the various commands we give the computer—for example, PRINT, READ, STOP, RUN, and so on.

So a single bit of information is one unit of a binary number, either 0 or 1. When the computer uses the four bits 1010 to stand for decimal 10, or when it uses some other combination of binary bits to stand for a letter of the alphabet, we call that binary expression a *byte*. So while 1 and 0 are bits, the binary expression 010111 stands for the byte W. Now a computer word such as PRINT or GOTO obviously will be made up of a much larger number of bits than a single character of the alphabet. With only these three classes of binary numbers—bits, bytes, and words—a computer can carry out all its complex computations, from adding 1 + 1 to guiding a spacecraft across hundreds of millions of kilometers of space.

CODING INFORMATION FOR COMPUTER MEMORY

To prevent a computer from having the electronic equivalent of a nervous breakdown, the binary information fed to it must be well organized by humans. We have already seen how digits are translated into binary numbers. For reasons that will be made clear in a moment, we add zeros to the left of each of the 0 through 9 binary numbers to provide each binary group with six digits, like this:

Decimal number	Binary number	Binary code for computer
0	0	000000
1	1	000001
2	10	000010
3	11	000011
4	100	000100
5	101	000101
6	110	000110
7	111	000111
8	1000	001000
9	1001	001001

We can also assign a set of binary code digits for each character of the alphabet, like this:

Character	Binary code for computer
A	110001
B	110010
C	110011
D	110100
E	110101
F	110110
G	110111
H	111000
I	111001
J	100001
K	100010
L	100011
M	100100
N	100101
O	100110
P	100111
Q	101000
R	101001
S	010010
T	010011
U	010100
V	010101
W	010110
X	010111
Y	011000
Z	011001

Punctuation marks are also binary-coded for the machine so that a computer keyboard has a total of 64 sets of machine-coded binary digits—10 for the numbers 0 through 9, 26 for the characters of the alphabet, and an additional 28 for punctuation marks and abbreviation signs. Notice that the alphabet characters are broken down into three groups—A through I; J through R; and S through Z. Notice also that A through I are coded by beginning each six-digit binary code group with 11. Following the 11 in each case is the binary code group for the decimals 1 through 9, so that C, the third letter of the alphabet, is made up of 11 + the binary code group for decimal 3, or 11 + 0011, or 110011. G becomes 11 + 0111, or 110111, and so on.

Now notice that the alphabet characters J through R are differently coded. The first two digits in the binary code group are not 11, but 10. Then as with the characters A through I, the characters J through R are given the binary code groups for the decimals 1 through 9. S through Z are similarly coded, but the first two binary digits here are 01. So the total of 64 characters (numbers, letters, and punctuation and abbreviation signs) are translated into computer number-language as 64 six-number binary code groups made up of 0s and 1s. Even at this early stage of looking into a computer's memory, it is very clear that all the information fed into a computer for memorizing is very highly *structured*.

To make things even simpler for the computer we add two more digits in front of each six-digit group so that each group ends up with a total of eight digits. Whenever the first digit in a given group is a 1, this means that the character in question forms the first character of the word in question. Or it can mean that the character in question is a one-character word. When the first digit is a 0 the computer then knows that the character in question is not the first character in a given word, or that it is not a one-letter word. This first digit in the eight-digit binary group serves as a space indicator between letters so that word patterns are formed; for example, so that the computer will print EVERY NOW AND THEN, instead of EV-ERYNOWANDTHEN.

The second of the two digits we have just added to our six-digit group serves as a way of detecting errors. Again, to keep things as simple (structured) as possible for our dumb but lightning-fast computer, we provide each binary code group with an even number of 1s. So the letter "W" in the word "WHERE" would be coded as 10 010110. But the "W" in the word "AWAY" would be coded as 01 010110. The machine has been instructed, through its design, never to accept a binary code group with an odd number of 1s. If we try to sneak such a code group past the computer, it signals "!ERROR."

We have chosen one of the simpler ways of coding information for a computer's use. It is the language used by the IBM Model 1401 computer and is called the Model 1401 eight-bit machine code. Although there are other computer languages, Model 1401 serves our purposes here, which are to show how information entering a computer's sensory-information store is coded, or structured, and then filed away in the computer's memory for later association and recall. The information entering our human sensory-information store also is coded. The way it is coded depends on whether it arrives through our eyes, ears, nose, or skin. It then enters our short-term memory and, depending on how well we rehearse and structure it, then enters our long-term memory. As you can conclude by now, in the case of computers we know more about how information is processed and memorized than we do in humans.

Fortunately, the operator of a computer does not have to encode data into binary digit groups for computer digestion and processing. When the operator punches the B key of the computer keyboard, electrical signals translate the action into the binary code group for B. Whether or not the operator presses the keyboard space bar signals whether the first digit in the eight-digit binary code group for B is a 0 or a 1. The computer then automatically registers a 1 or 0 as the second digit in the code group to provide an even number of 1s.

In the reverse process, bits, bytes, and words can be recalled from the computer's memory store and printed on paper or flashed onto a video display screen by the computer operator. If the words are specially coded computer words, such as COMPARE, READ, PUNCH, MCS, (for "move characters and suppress zeroes"), all we have to do if we don't know their meaning is look up the meaning in the computer code book. Computers are very particular about recognizing one and only one very precise meaning to each word in their vocabulary. It is impossible for a computer to be vague by dishing up fuzzy meanings to words.

Now that you have seen how information must first be coded before a computer can deal with it, let's find out how the computer retains a given code group in its electronic memory store.

THE COMPUTER MEMORY

A computer's millions upon millions of bits of information are stored in memory "cells." Several bits make up a larger unit of information called a *byte*. Each bit has what is called an *address*, or physical location somewhere within the computer's circuits, although the byte usually is the smallest addressable unit. You have to do acrobatics to address bits, but it can be done.

One of the many marvels of our electronic age is that tiny, cell-like component of a computer called a *chip*. Made of silicon, a chip only a few millimeters on a side is capable of storing more than 64,000 bits! Chips manage this seemingly mountainous task by having an electric circuit network arranged in a grid consisting of columns and rows. In the example shown here, we have simplified matters by using an imaginary chip with only 64 memory cells. One bit of information can be stored in each memory-cell location, or intersection of columns and rows. This means that we can feed into the computer's memory bank, which consists of many, many memory storage chips, one or more bits or bytes of information and know the exact address (memory cell) of

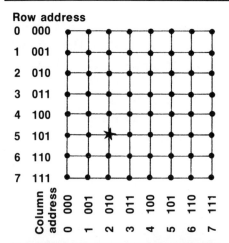

Row address

In this computer memory cell with 64 locations, one bit of information (the star) is stored in the form of an electrical charge located at the intersection of Row 5 and Column 2.

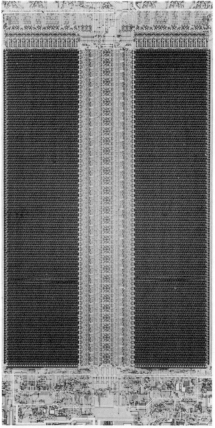

This computer memory chip has storage locations for 16,384 bits. It measures only 2.8 by 5.1 millimeters, which is about the size of the letter "M". COURTESY OF MOSTEK CORPORATION.

each. Since we know the address of a given bit, at a later time we can retrieve it. At the same time we can retrieve several other bits, which when combined might form the word "CONGRATULATIONS" or the numerical answer to a complex math problem, such as working out the value of *pi* to 100,000 places, which a computer has done, by the way.

The location of a given bit is given by two binary numbers, one for the row and the other for the column. In the case shown here, the row location of our bit is 101, or the third row up from the bottom. The column location is 010, or the sixth column from the right. Our single bit of information may be in the form of a tiny electric charge (1) temporarily stored in the memory cell, or it may be in the form of no charge (0). So a bit of computer information coded in binary form is either a tiny electric charge (1) or the lack of an electric charge (0) at a given chip location. Now imagine not one chip but numerous stacks of chips that can store many millions of bits of information. That is the picture of the memories inside today's computers.

FAST MEMORIES, SLOW MEMORIES

There are different kinds of computer memories. All are accurate but some are faster or larger than others. Which kind of computer memory we want depends on how much money we are willing to spend. A simple and inexpensive computer memory is a cassette tape like those used in relatively inexpensive home microcomputers. An average cassette tape has a memory store of one million to ten million bits.

A tape that winds onto one reel from another and back again is not a very efficient way to store information for rapid recall. What if you want to retrieve several bytes of information midway along the tape right after the tape has just completed rewinding itself back to 0, the beginning? To get at the information you must advance the tape at fast-forward and then stop it at the wanted location. Retrieving information in this way from a moving cassette tape takes from ten to a hundred seconds, known in computer language as *memory access time.*

When you play a cassette tape the tape moves across a magnetic head—the PLAY head—of the tape recorder. The PLAY command given to a tape recorder simply tells the recorder to recall and present the information stored on its tape-memory. In a computer, the command READ punched out on the computer's keyboard tells the computer to recall information from its memory. The command WRITE tells the computer to store the information just fed to it. The command RECORD on a tape recorder is similar to the command WRITE for a computer. In both RECORD and WRITE instances we are adjusting the machine so that we may feed information into its memory for later retrieval.

An improvement over a cassette tape memory is a memory that involves a disc similar to a phonograph record. When you play a phonograph record the stylus picks up mechanical vibrations in the long, continuous groove of the record. It translates those vibrations into electrical impulses that are then converted by a speaker into air vibrations that we hear as sound. By moving the stylus arm to any position on the record we can instantly hear what we want, provided that we know where on the record it is stored.

The disc memory of a computer operates in a similar way. The main difference is that in place of grooves on the record, the disc contains a thin film of magnetic material, like that covering the play/record surface of a magnetic tape. When the magnetic heads of a disc memory are told to find certain bytes of information stored on the spinning disc they go instantly to the track, or groove, where the wanted information is stored. This system is far more rapid than a tape storage memory. A typical magnetic disc has about 800 tracks on each side and each track can store 100,000 bits. So a total of 160 million bits can be stored on one disc. The average access time to a given memory address is about 20 milliseconds. One advantage of tapes and discs is that they can be filled with information that we want to keep and use over and over again and then can be removed from the computer and filed away in a filing cabinet (inactive memory bank) for later use.

One of the most rapid memory-recall devices around is called the CCD (which stands for "charge-coupled device"). It consists of a single chip measuring 4.4 by 5.8 millimeters. On this chip are 16 grids each of which contains 4,096 memory cells and, therefore, the same number of bits. So the entire chip contains a total of 65,536 memory cells. What makes this chip different from the first one we described is that the information bits stored at each memory-cell location are not stationary. Instead, all 4,096 bits stored in each grid of memory cells are circulating around their particular grid. Further, the circulation patterns and time are identical for each grid. It is as if the information stored on each grid were moving continuously through a closed pipeline. Whenever the computer is told to retrieve certain bits of information from its memory cells it is as if the computer were able to reach out and grab the wanted bits as they fly by. So rapidly are the information bits circulating around a given grid that the computer's access time with the CCD memory is only 0.5 millisecond. But what if the solution to a problem requires the retrieval of a few million bits of information? All those tiny fractions of a second for the retrieval of each bit, and then its association with other bits into bytes, can add up to minutes and hours.

The fastest memory retrieval system yet invented is called the RAM, which stands for *random-access memory*. In RAM there is no mechanical device that has to locate an address of a given bit. And the information stored in the magnetic memory cells of a RAM device is not circulating in order to cut down the length of time it takes for the computer to reach out and "grab it" as it goes by. Instead, retrieval of a given bit, no matter what its address on the memory chip, occurs in about 200 nanoseconds (a nanosecond is one billionth of a second). The RAM system is the one we started with back on page 61 when we explained how binary bits are stored in memory cells of a memory chip coated with a thin magnetic film and then later retrieved as bytes at an electronic address.

COMPUTER MEMORY vs. HUMAN MEMORY

Let's compare a computer memory with our human memory in a meaningful way. Inventing artificial memories capable of competing with the human brain just might give neuroscientists insights into the human brain which they might not otherwise have. A science, called cybernetics, has grown up around this idea since the late 1940s.

The most reliable estimates we have of the number of synapses in the human brain (junctions where neurons come in contact with one another) come to about 10 trillion. Now if we assume that each synapse of the brain can handle one bit of information, then the total bits the human brain can hold is 10 trillion bits. That is a lot of bits, particularly when you consider that all of them can be stored in a space as small as the human skull, which measures about 1,375 cubic centimeters. Since we have those two figures handy, let's come up with an important third one by dividing 10 trillion storage units by 1,000 cubic centimeters (rounded off from 1,375) of storage space and getting the number of stored units occupying a given storage space. The calculation shows that the human brain is able to store 10 billion bits per cubic centimeter compared with the computer's ability to store only one million bits per cubic centimeter. According to IBM computer scientist Lewis M. Branscomb, a mere twenty-five years ago "a computer memory packing this much information would have filled a small mountain 500 meters high." At the present time the human brain's capacity to store information is ten thousand times greater than that of the big computers today.

Let's look at still another figure, one dealing with how much information your brain and mine are capable of processing and storing. If on the average my brain processes about 25 bits of information per second, and has done so since I was born, then by the time I reach age sixty-five I will have processed about 50 billion bits. Let's assume also that I have that rare ability of total recall, which I don't, and that I can remember and have accessible in memory storage all 50 billion bits. The amazing figure we now come up with is this: I am left with the lion's share (well over 9 trillion) of my total number of bit storage sites, or synapses, unused, reserved for the daily business of processing information in decision making. Surely this puts the smartest and fastest computer to shame, or should.

But what about the rates at which the computer and human brain can process information? Our fastest computers today, using RAM, can process in only an hour the entire input-output information flow of a human being's lifetime! Even "slow" computers of the 1980s are at least a million times faster at processing information than the human brain. And that figure is bound to increase a lot before the end of this decade.

The question we now want to ask is this: Is it easier to program the human brain to catch up with the computer in those areas where the computer is superior? Or is it easier to design computers to catch up with the human brain in those areas where the human brain is superior? To put the question another way: Do we use the computer as a model for improving the human brain? Or do we use the human brain as a model for improving the computer? It seems that a little bit of each might be in order. But we would be in a much better position to improve the computer, on the basis of a human-brain model to copy, if we knew more about the human brain!

At first glance the question of improving the human brain might seem ridiculous. How can we possibly change the human brain to give it this or that desirable aspect of a smart and/or fast computer? In the long run the question might not be as ridiculous as it seems. One logical place to search in the human memory system is the structure and chemical composition of a human neuron. A neural impulse is an electrochemical event that travels along a nerve at the maximum rate of about a hundred meters per second. Compare this with the rate at which a computer "neural impulse" travels—the speed of light, which is three million times faster than a human neural impulse. It would seem that evolution has fixed the rate at which nerve impulses travel through our human tissues, for they do not change from one human being to another. Increasing the speed of human nerve impulses would be one way to meet the challenge of the electronic computer. But this approach seems fruitless. Is there another, and workable, way of "programming" the human brain to mimic certain admirable aspects of the computer?

BIOLOGICAL MEMORY CELLS FOR COMPUTERS

What are the possibilities of copying certain biological systems and designing them into a computer to increase the computer's memory? Branscomb thinks that computer engineers are nearing the end of a dead-end street as they keep improving the computer's memory cell as it is now known. He says that they must come up with something entirely different from anything known today in computer technology. What he envisions is a three-dimensional memory cell that has the ability to reproduce more memory cells like itself. Is there such a memory cell in existence today? Of course, the DNA (deoxyribonucleic acid) molecule. This remarkable molecule is present in living organisms. It carries the genetic code determining that the offspring of two parents will have certain traits—eye and hair color, for example—of its parents. DNA does this by being able to make exact copies of itself, copies that are transferred from parent to offspring.

According to Branscomb, a single molecule of DNA, which is far smaller than the smallest computer memory cell yet engineered, can store ten billion bits of information. "Before the next 100 years are up," he says, "we will probably have to build a biological crystal computer out of something like DNA; in short, we may have to reinvent the brain."

It would seem, then, that we can learn much from biological systems as we attempt to improve computers. But whether we are able to improve human memory and learning by artificial means remains to be seen. One thing is certain, however. The computer's memory and learning ability are bound to improve by leaps and bounds over the next several years. How will supercomputers of the next few decades change our lives?

First, engineers tell us that microcomputers will be the size of a book and smaller. Book-size computers could have the advantage of a videoscreen image larger than the image projected onto the screen of a miniature pocket computer. This new generation of computers will be able to do everything the most sophisticated pocket calculators can do today and will have memories millions of times more efficient. It will be a simple matter, at the push of a button, to tie in with very smart and very fast computers elsewhere—orbiting satellite-computers, computers located in public and university libraries, grocery stores, and elsewhere. Printed railway and bus timetables will no longer be needed. Your computer will not only tell you when the next train for Larchmont is scheduled to depart, but it will tell you how late it is at a given moment. City maps may also become things of the past. If you are exploring a new city, a satellite computer will project onto your videoscreen an image of a street plan of the city, or of any small part of it. The image will be up to date as of the moment you push the command button.

Mathematical tables of all kinds, including conversions from one unit of measure to another, will be at your fingertips. So will instant translations from one language into any other language. This expanded ability of the supercomputers of the near future will depend on two things: (1) a greatly expanded memory store; and (2) instant access to specialized memory stores located in many countries. When such a time comes our education system very likely will undergo reorganization. But we will have to become more experienced in deciding which aspects of human knowledge to store in the memories of computers and which aspects are better handled by the human brain.

6

HOW TO
IMPROVE
YOUR MEMORY

If you want to remember something, make up a story about it, or invent a picture of it. That, in a nutshell, is at the root of practically all the techniques used by people who have become professional memory artists, or *mnemonists*, those skilled in the art of memory, called *mnemonics*. There is no better example of this approach than the remarkable Russian mnemonist who is known in psychological literature simply as Mr. S.

S was a journalist who had no idea that his truly remarkable memory was different from that of anyone else. When eventually he did discover that his memory was so well developed that he had no known equal, he became a stage performer. S was able to memorize a complex table of numbers in a matter of minutes and then recall the table, without error, years later. He had no trouble remembering anything he experienced. His problem turned out to be learning to forget.

What was the secret of this man's remarkable memory? He did not employ any "tricks" that could be called cheating. His photographic memory came quite naturally to him. Over the years the workings of his memory were revealed bit by bit as he subjected himself to about thirty years of experiments conducted by the famous Soviet pyschologist, A. R. Luria. S first came to Luria's attention in the 1920s when S was working as a newspaper reporter. His editor read off long and detailed assignments to his staff of reporters each morning. The editor had become increasingly annoyed day after day on noticing that S never took notes while everyone else did.

One morning the editor asked S why he never took notes, saying that note taking was the mark of a good reporter. S said that there was no need because he remembered everything, whereupon he repeated his long assignment word for word. So impressed was the editor that he asked S if he would be willing to see a psychologist and have his memory tested. That is how S came to the attention of Luria, and so began their long association.

There is perhaps no better example on record of right-hemisphere dominance in an individual than in this remarkable case. Pleasing images, frightening images, hilarious images, sad images, tragic images, an endless association of images became the pegs of S's memory store. And they were images that simply came to him without energy on his part. Further, the images were wrapped in odors, colors, had weight, texture, and often were associated with sounds. He was able to move these images about in new associations at will. He could make them larger, smaller, darker, or lighter. Each individual image served as a memory peg for a number, a word, an object which had entered S's experience. At one time S described how he regarded numbers:

THE "PERSONALITY" OF NUMBERS

"For me 2, 4, 6, 5 are not just numbers. They have forms. 1 is a pointed number—which has nothing to do with the way it's written. It's because it's somehow firm and complete. 2 is flatter, rectangular, whitish in color, sometimes almost a gray. 3 is a pointed segment which rotates. 4 is also square and dull; it looks like 2 but has more substance to it, it's thicker. 5 is absolutely complete and takes the form of a cone or a tower—something substantial. 6, the first number after 5, has a whitish hue; 8 somehow has a naive quality, it's milky blue like lime. . . ."

At another time he had this to say about numbers reminding him of images:

"Take the number 1. This is a proud, well-built man; 2 is a high-spirited woman; 3, a gloomy person (why I don't know); 6, a man with a swollen foot; 7, a man with a mustache; 8, a very stout woman—a sack within a sack. As for the number 87, what I see is a fat woman and a man twirling his mustache."

When S memorized tables of numbers he either converted all the individual numbers into individual images which he then associated, or he simply mentally "photographed" the entire table. For example, he memorized the following table, according to Luria, in two and a half to three minutes.

6680	1002
5432	3451
1684	7935
2768	1926
4237	2967
3891	5520

At the end of that time S was able to recite the entire table in any order he was asked to—by columns, rows, forward, or backward. He could begin anywhere and recall the numbers in sequence either forward or backward. Even more remarkable, fifteen years later when asked to recall the table he did so with only a moment's pause and without an error.

S recognized words not as we do but by the images this or that word evoked, images blending sight, sound, and odor. Scientists call the ability of one sense to stimulate other senses *synesthesia,* which was extremely keen in S. Here is how he described it:

THE "TASTE" OF WORDS

"I recognize a word not only by the images it evokes but by a whole complex of feelings that an image arouses. It's hard to express . . . it's not a matter of vision or hearing but some overall sense I get. Usually I experience a word's taste and weight, and I don't have to make an effort to remember it—the word seems to recall itself. But it's difficult to describe. What I sense is something oily slipping through my hand . . . or I'm aware of a slight tickling in my left hand caused by a mass of tiny, lightweight points. When that happens I simply remember, without having to make the attempt. . . ."

As Luria pointed out, the *visual* quality of his recall was at the base of his ability to remember words. Whenever S was asked to memorize a list of words he would take an imaginary walk along a street he knew very well and would hang one word on a fence post, another on a street lamp, another in a shop window, and so on to the end of the list. To recall the list forward or backward he would repeat his stroll picking each word as he came to it off its memory peg. Sometimes he would omit a word from a list. However, the word had not been "forgotten," rather he had missed seeing the image of it during his stroll of recall down the familiar street. Here is how S himself explained omitting the word *pencil*, the word *egg*, the word *blimp*, and the word *banner* in four different word lists:

"I put the image of the **pencil** near the fence . . . the one down the street, you know. But what happened was that the image fused with that of the fence and I walked right on past without noticing it. The same thing happened with the word **egg.** I had put it up against a white wall and it blended in with the background. How could I possibly spot a white egg up against a white wall? Now that word **blimp.** That's something gray, so it blended in with the gray of the pavement. . . . **Banner,** of course, means the Red Banner. But, you know, the building which houses the Moscow City Soviet of Workers'

Deputies is also red, and since I'd put the banner close to one of the walls of the building I just walked on without seeing it. . . . Sometimes I put a word in a dark place and have trouble seeing it as I go by."

So S's "forgetting" wasn't forgetting at all; it really was a temporary oversight, or lack of concentration. Later, when he was performing memory feats on the stage, he deliberately worked on his images, making them more vivid and simplifying them. He described his improvements:

"[The one thing] I do now is to make my images larger. Take the word egg I told you about before. It was so easy to lose sight of it; now I make it a larger image, and when I lean it up against the wall of a building, I see to it that the place is lit up by having a street lamp nearby. . . . I don't put things in dark passageways any more. . . . Much better if there's some light around; it's easier to spot them."

And on simplifying his images:

"Formerly, in order to remember a thing, I would have to summon up an image of the whole scene. Now all I have to do is take some detail I've decided on in advance that will signify the whole image. Say I'm given the word *horseman*. All it takes now is an image of a foot in a spur."

As a professional mnemonist, S often would be given passages to remember in a language unknown by him, or complex math equations, or simply a list of nonsense syllables. For instance, he was once given several lines in Italian from *The Divine Comedy*, the first two lines of which read:

Nel mezzo del cammin di nostra vita
Mi ritrovai per una selva oscura

Here is how S quickly memorized them and recited them back accurately, with the correct accent and intonations. His only requirement for memorizing such meaningless (to him) sound combinations was that each word be pronounced clearly and slowly and with a brief pause between words. Here is how he did it:

"(*Nel*) I was paying my membership dues when there, in the

corridor, I caught sight of the ballerina **Nel'** skaya.

"(*mezzo*) I myself am a violinist; what I do is to set up an image of a man together with [Russian: **vmeste**] Nel'skaya, who is playing the violin.

"(*del*) There's a pack of **Deli** cigarettes near them.

"(*cammin*) I set up an image of a fireplace [Russian: **dver**].

"(*nostra*) I see a nose [Russian: **nos**]; a man has tripped and, in falling, gotten his nose pinched in the doorway (**tra**).

"(*vita*) He lifts his leg over the threshold, for a child is lying there, that is, a sign of life—**vita**lism." And so on.

Here is how S recalled memorizing a complex mathematical equation. The one shown here, which is a meaningless one, was actually presented to him during one of his stage performances:

$$N \cdot \sqrt[3]{d^2 \times \frac{85}{vx}} \cdot \sqrt{\frac{276^2 \cdot 86x}{n^2v \cdot \pi 264}} \; n^3b = \delta v \frac{1624}{32^2} \cdot r^2s$$

"Neiman (**N**) came out and jabbed at the ground with his cane (**.**). He looked up at a tall tree which resembled the square-root sign ($\sqrt{}$), and thought to himself: 'No wonder the tree has withered and begun to expose its roots. After all, it was here when I built these two houses (**d²**).' Then he said: 'The houses are old, I'll have to get rid of them (**X**); the sale will bring in far more money.' He had originally invested 85,000 in them (**85**). Then I see the roof of the house detached (———), while down below on the street I see a man playing the termenvox (**vx**). He's standing near a mailbox, and on the corner there's a large stone (**.**). . . ." And so on.

At one of his performances, S was given the following list of nonsense syllables and successfully repeated them. Four years later, Luria asked S if he still remembered the list and S said that he did, whereupon he repeated the list and gave the following explanation of how he had initially memorized the nonsense syllables:

1. ma va na sa na va
2. na sa na ma va
3. sa na ma va na
4. va sa na va na ma
5. na va na va sa ma
6. na ma sa ma va na
7. sa ma sa va na
8. na sa ma va ma na

"Even though it's several years since I gave the performance," S began, "it's all so vivid, I can see it so clearly, that it seems more like a performance of four months ago rather than four years ago.

"[Once I realized that the words I was to memorize were nonsense syllables with only one vowel], I asked my assistant to read the first three words as a single unit, without breaking them down into syllables, [then to call out the next three syllables also as a unit and so down the list]. The monotonous repetition of the vowel *a* in each syllable helped to create a distinct rhythm and stress, so that the lines sounded like this: MAVÁ—NASÁ—NAVÁ. From this point on, I was able to reproduce the series without pausing, and at a good pace.

"This is the way I worked it out in my mind. My landlady (*MAVÁ*), whose house on Slizkaya Street I stayed at while I was in Warsaw, was leaning out of a window that opened onto a courtyard. With her left hand she was pointing inside, toward the room (*NASÁ*) [Russian: *nasha*, "our"]; while with her right she was making some negative gesture (*NAVÁ*) [Yiddish expression for "no"] to an old-clothes man who was standing in the yard with a sack slung over his right shoulder . . ." and so on.

Was S an exceptionally intelligent man? As a result of his gift for memory, we might be tempted to think that he was. It turned out that he was not. In fact, in several ways he was below average intelligence. For instance he was once given the following table of numbers to memorize:

```
1 2 3 4
2 3 4 5
3 4 5 6
4 5 6 7
    etc.
```

Without analyzing the table he memorized it by using his visual recall system. By so doing he put much more energy into the task than was necessary. All he need have done was notice that each successive line begins with a number one digit higher and that the beginning number of each line is followed by the next three higher numbers. Other such tests revealed that S simply did not have the ability to see a *logical* ordering of material, whether numbers or words, that could be easily associated.

While S's remarkable synesthetic ability enabled him to perform remarkable memory feats, it interfered with memory as most of us know it. For example, S had great difficulty remembering faces and voices. Faces, he said, are so changeable because each of us wears a different face depending on our moods. The different shades of expression on a given person's face did not serve to help S remember the face but actually confused him and made it hard for him to remember the face. He also said that his keen mingled senses enabled him to identify not one but numerous voices of a single individual. Each change in voice tone for S became a different voice, and he simply could not keep track of the many different voices any given friend had. A friend calling him when in a bright mood in the morning was unrecognized by S in the afternoon if the person called when in a state of gloom. S also could not relate the meanings of several lines of poetry, or the meaning of a short story, when such passages were read at a normal pace and with the reader's voice changing mood and intonation according to the feeling he interpreted in each line or sentence.

"No," S would say, "this is too much. Each word calls up

images; they collide with one another, and the result is chaos. I can't make anything out of this. And, then, there's also your voice . . . another blur . . . then everything's muddled." S had great difficulty understanding the main idea expressed by a mathematical formula or a stanza of poetry, although he could recite both formula and stanza, no matter how complex, unerringly. According to Luria, S was a prisoner in his world of images. He was never able to break out of the world and comprehend the larger meanings of words and phrases, meanings that lay beyond the scented, textured, and colored images.

EIDETIC IMAGES

When S re-created an image of a table of numbers or of a familiar street down which he strolled and placed various items he wished to remember, the image that aided him was one called an *eidetic* image; that is, an image seen outside of the viewer, not inside the viewer's head. A number of people with the ability to create eidetic images have been studied by psychologists. One such study was done by Ralph Norman Haber, of the University of Rochester, who studied numerous eidetic children. Here is part of a tape-recorded conversation with a ten-year-old boy who reported eidetic images. The boy sat before a painting from *Alice in Wonderland* and studied the painting for a while; then the painting was removed. As the experimenter asked questions the boy remained seated and looked at a blank screen on which he said he saw an image of the picture he had just been studying.

Experimenter: Do you see something there?

Boy: I see the tree, gray tree with three limbs. I see the cat with stripes around its tail.

Experimenter: Can you count those stripes?

Boy: Yes (pause). There's about sixteen.

Experimenter: You're counting what? Black, white or both?

Boy: Both.

Experimenter: Tell me what else you see.

Boy: And I can see the flowers on the bottom. There's about three stems, but you can see two pairs of flowers. One on the right has green leaves, red flower on bottom with yellow on top. And I can see the girl with a green dress. She's got blonde hair and a red hair band and there are some leaves in the upper left-hand corner where the tree is.

Experimenter: Can you tell me about the roots of the tree?

Boy: Well, there's two of them going down here [points] and there's one that cuts off on the left-hand side of the picture.

Experimenter: What is the cat doing with its paws?

Boy: Well, one of them he's holding out and the other one is on the tree.

Experimenter: What color is the sky?

Boy: Can't tell.

Experimenter: Can't tell at all?

Boy: No. I can see the yellowish ground, though.

Experimenter: Tell me if any of the parts go away or change at all as I'm talking to you. What color is the girl's dress?

Boy: Green. It has some white on it.

Experimenter: How about her legs and feet?

(The boy looks away from the screen and then back again.)

Experimenter: Is the image gone?

Boy: Yes, except for the tree.

Experimenter: Tell me when it goes away.

Boy: (pause) It went away.

Are such "photographic memories" real in that an eidetic person actually sees an image outside his head and can describe details of the image as he sees them, as opposed to remembering them from the real picture? Haber says that details associated with an eidetic image are different from remembered details. The first are actually seen while the second details are recalled from the individual's memory store. Haber says that numerous times eidetic children have told him that they *remember* this or that detail from the picture but that they can *see* details that they can't remember. When asked to move their eidetic image from one surface to another, says Haber, almost all the children tested said that the image falls off the edge of the surface and is lost.

There is the case of a nineteen-year-old college student who has a remarkable ability to remember pictorial material. She can study a painting for about thirty seconds and after it is removed describe it in great detail. But the image she has of the painting is not eidetic. Instead the image is remembered and occurs inside her head, not "out there." As she recalls details from the painting, her eyes do not scan this way and that in search of the details. All of us have this ability to a certain extent, but this girl's ability to duplicate a painting in her imagination is far better developed than that in most of us.

OTHER MNEMONISTS

There are other mnemonists, and each seems to have his or her special techniques of memory. For example, A. C. Aitken was a mathematics professor at the University of Edinburgh, Scotland. He was known as a lightning calculator with numbers and also had a remarkable memory for facts. He had memorized the value of *pi* to 1,000 places! But he described the feat as being "reprehensibly useless, had it not been so easy." He also once memorized a list of twenty-five unrelated words and twenty-seven years later was able to recite the list without an error. While most of us can remember a sequence of five to nine digits, if they are read off to us slowly, Aitken could remember sequences of fifteen read to him at the rate of five digits per second. He said that his talent to memorize numbers quickly and easily came from his many years of working with numbers as a mathematician and his superior knowledge of relationships among numbers. For example, he once said that he could remember the sequence 1961 as 37×53, also as $44^2 + 5^2$, and as $40^2 + 19^2$.

Then there is the case of the college student who had the remarkable ability of talking backward. On hearing or being shown the word "envelope," for instance, she immediately was able to say *epolevne*, not that it did her much good, mind you. She also reportedly could repeat short sentences backward, provided they did not contain more than about nine words. When tested, this girl scored below normal in her ability to handle graphic images. For instance, she was studying ballet but continually had trouble keeping a clear image in her mind of where the other dancers were on the stage at a given time. She also had a poor sense of direction and had difficulty forming a mental map of the area where she lived.

Contrast this college student's inferior ability to create graphic images with the outstanding ability of the mnemonist V.P., who was studied by E. Hunt and T. Love. V.P. learned to read when he was only three and a half years old. By the age of five he had memorized the street map of a large city (of 500,000 population). By the age of eight he was a skilled chess player. At the age of ten he memorized 150 poems as part of a contest.

It would be possible to describe the feats of still more mnemonists but there is no need. We would find that nearly all mnemonists studied have two chief things in common: (1) most have the ability to create rich visual images of one sort or another, of a street scene or a table of numbers, in the case of S, for example; (2) most also have the ability to produce a rich network of meaningful associations, either with visual images or with words not associated with visual images, as in the case of the college student who can talk backward.

WHY STUDY MNEMONICS?

For hundreds of years mnemonics as an art, and mnemonists as exceptional people, were very popular subjects. Before printing was invented, before cheap writing materials were easily available, and before the general public was taught to read and write, the ability to memorize large amounts of material was very important. So it was natural for any person with an unusual ability to memorize large amounts of material to be singled out for praise and admiration.

The importance placed on mnemonic skills began to decline as more and more people learned to read and write and cheap writing materials became available. Why bother to memorize a long shopping list, for example, when it could be written down and carried to market? And why bother to memorize certain number tables when they could be looked up in an inexpensive book? Many young people today are annoyed at having to learn how to do square-root problems, for instance, when all they have to do to find the square root of a number is punch a button on their pocket calculator. So gradually, mnemonics lost its appeal, at least among scholars, and mnemonists began to be looked upon as little more than sideshow freaks. The subject really never lost its popular appeal, however. In recent years it has attracted the interest of psychologists and neuroscientists who are interested in learning how our natural memory works. Says Baddeley of mnemonic systems: "They reflect the same basic processes that underlie normal unaided memory. They reflect some of these processes particularly clearly, as in the case of visual memory." And as other psychologists have said about the wave of new academic interest in mnemonic systems, be they magic or gimmick, they really do work. Psychologist Gordon Bower, of Stanford University, says that college students using the "loci" system of memory (see below) tend to remember seven times more than do other students relying on free recall or memory systems of their own that do not involve "loci."

MNEMONIC SYSTEM OF PLACES, OR "LOCI"

The oldest known mnemonic system is the one used so successfully by S. It is called the system of places, or *loci*, which is the Latin word for "places" (singular, *locus*). The invention of the *loci* system is credited to the Greek poet

Simonides, who lived around 500 B.C., as reported by the Roman statesman Cicero, who lived around 50 B.C. According to Cicero's account, a nobleman by the name of Scopas employed Simonides to recite a poem in praise of him at a banquet. Simonides did so, but in the poem included praise also for the twin gods Castor and Pollux. Annoyed because Simonides had not devoted the entire poem to him, Scopas said that he would pay Simonides only half the agreed fee and that he would have to collect the rest of his fee from the gods he so highly praised!

Midway through the banquet a messenger came up to Simonides and said that two callers were waiting outside to see him. On going outside, Simonides found no one and was about to return to the banquet when the roof of the building caved in and killed all those in the banquet hall. The bodies of all the guests were crushed beyond recognition, so the story goes. When relatives of the dead came to claim the bodies they could not tell one from another. Simonides came to the rescue and identified every corpse in the banquet hall. He was able to do this because he had a clear image of where each guest had been sitting during dinner. It was through his memory of the *places* occupied by the guests that Simonides was able to identify the corpses. The remaining half of Simonides' fee was an important half indeed—his life—paid by his two callers.

Those wanting to train their memory, said Simonides, "must select places and form mental images of the things they want to remember and store those images in the places. In that way the order of the places will keep the order of the things, and the images of the things will call up the things themselves."

When you use the *loci* system of mnemonics you will, of course, have to memorize a whole series of memory pegs, or *loci*, in sequence. It is essential that the *loci* form a series and be remembered in order. You may have to work several days or weeks, depending how long your *loci* series is, until you have it memorized without a flaw. It is a good idea to begin with a short list, say of ten *loci*, then enlarge it gradually until you have fifty or a hundred or more items. It is essential that the items in your series be in a given order so that you can easily rehearse and recite to yourself any part of the list either forward, backward, or from any *locus* in the series forward or backward. Once you have memorized a set of *loci*, you can use them forever. If you happen to be interested in astrology, why not start building a *loci* system around the twelve signs of the Zodiac? One scholar of classical Greece, named Metrodorus, did just that and ended up with 360 loci which he reportedly put to very good use in many ways.

Suppose that you have memorized a sequence of fifty *loci* and that you ask people at a gathering to start calling off objects at the rate of one every two seconds until all fifty of your *loci* are occupied. You then review your *loci*, just as S used to stroll down his familiar street, and call off the objects correctly in any order you may be asked. But what if someone asks you to start with object number 25 and proceed backward to object number 12 and then stop? A quick way of doing this is to accent, or in some way underline, every fifth object in your list so that you can go immediately to any of these key objects and know its number in sequence. Suppose, for instance, that the first 10 objects in your list were (1) plant stand; (2) marble tabletop; (3) spiral staircase; (4) hi-fi cabinet (in which there is a) (5) turntable well (and a) (6) tape-recorder well; (7) fireplace; (8) mantle above the fireplace; (9) wood box; and (10) loudspeaker enclosure. How would you accent turntable well and speaker enclosure in order to remember that they are objects number 5 and 10 respectively?

One way would be to envision five turntables and ten loudspeakers. Another way would be to memorize a second short list such as lead, tin, copper, silver, gold, platinum, each metal in the series more valuable than the previous one. That would be your key to remembering their proper sequence. Let lead signify the object number 5 in your base list, tin object number 10, copper object number 15, silver, object number 20, and so on. Now you refine your base list of *loci* by envisioning a *lead* turntable, a loudspeaker enclosure with a *tin* sound, and so on.

What kinds of objects should you choose to form your base list of *loci?* Psychologists today say that the advice given in a book called *Ad Herennium* is as sound today as it was in ancient times when it was written:

> We ought, then, to set up images of a kind that can adhere longest in the memory. And we shall do so if we establish likenesses as striking as possible, if we set up images that are not so many or vague, but doing something; if we assign to them exceptional beauty or singular ugliness, if we dress some of them with crowns or purple cloaks, for example, so that the likeness may be more distinct to us; or if we somehow disfigure them, as by introducing one stained with blood . . . so that its form is more striking, or by assigning certain comic effects to our images, for that too will ensure our remembering them more readily. (*Ad Herennium*, III, xxii. xxxvii)

So as you carefully select items for your base list, try to select vivid, distinctive, active, grotesque, and comic images; in short, images that are easy to remember simply because they are so striking in some way, *any* way that works best for you. Psychologists are agreed that the list that works best is one that you make up yourself, not one that has been made up by someone else. So beware of "easy," instant, ready-made lists.

Now let's look at two different situations and apply them to the sample base list just given. That list, by the way, happens to represent the sequence in which furniture is arranged in one of my rooms, so the images are not grotesque, comic, or active. But they will serve to make the point. Say that the first four objects I want to memorize are microscope, flyswatter, compass, and bass fiddle. What I am going to do is form associations by pairing off the objects to be memorized with the first four objects in my base list, as follows:

(1) plant stand	microscope
(2) marble tabletop	flyswatter
(3) spiral staircase	compass
(4) hi-fi cabinet	bass fiddle

As the pairing is being done, here's what goes on in my imagination: First I see a **microscope** on the plant stand and a cactus plant is growing out of the microscope eyepiece. Second I see a gooey mess on my beautiful marble tabletop, the remains of a gigantic fly I have just smashed with the **flyswatter**. Third I see myself having an awful time trying to find out how my spiral staircase is oriented by using a **compass**. Fourth, try as I do I am unable to fit the **bass fiddle** into my hi-fi cabinet, and so on. Now you should be able to see why it is important to create in your imagination vivid and memorable images—because you will remember them quickly and easily. Using the above first four items of the sample base list of *loci,* pair the following four objects to be memorized and make up the most striking sequence of visual images that you can.

When you decide to draw up a base list of *loci* of your own, start small, say, with only ten objects. Experiment with three or four different lists to find out what kinds of base-list words you are having the most success with. Later in this chapter you will find important help in drawing up a different kind of base list. Once you have such a list drawn up, don't forget what was said in Chapter 3 about the importance of rehearsal in transferring information from your short-term memory into your long-term memory. So whenever you find yourself daydreaming while riding on a bus or walking, concentrate and rehearse your list. Rehearse it forward, backward, from item 5 through item 25 back to item 12, and so on. You will have mastered the list only when you are able to recite it in any way you wish just about as rapidly as you can count. In short, try to overlearn it. You'll be surprised at how quickly you will be able to put such a well-thought-out list to good use. Then it will be up to you to find ways of using the list. You should find many, the least important of which will be to amuse friends.

A second situation, and a useful one, in which a base list of *loci* can be used might be one similar to the following. Suppose the head of the school board is to deliver a speech in your local school. He decides not to use notes, instead relying on a mnemonic system of *loci*. As he rehearses his speech, first he must remember to greet the superintendent and others attending the meeting. Then he must remember to speak on ten major topics, the first three of which are (1) the gym's needing a new floor; (2) the football team's needing new uniforms; and (3) the science lab's needing new sinks.

Here are the images that fix the topics in order, in his memory:

(1) plant stand   greet superintendent and guests
(2) marble tabletop   gym needs new floor
(3) spiral staircase   football team needs new uniforms
(4) hi-fi cabinet   science lab needs new sinks

First, he envisions the superintendent sitting on the plant stand with a big grin on his face and waving at being greeted. So after greeting the superintendent with a few opening words, he simply continues on to greet the teachers, parents, and other guests. Second, the marble tabletop has suddenly become a superfloor for the gym, all gleaming and cold and hard. Third, the spiral staircase is a very busy place since all the members of the football team are running up and down it, and they are dressed only in their shorts, so they had better be given new uniforms. Fourth, the poor hi-fi cabinet: both the turntable well and tape-recorder well are filled up with water and are leaking; the water is dripping down into the record-storage area and getting the records all wet. And so on. Such vivid images are bound to work and make it unnecessary to use notes.

The reason they work so well is found in the interference theory of forgetting. In brief, when our memories fail it is often because unwanted items of memory interfere with those items we are trying to recall. Forgetting is not necessarily due to the mere passage of time. We may have trouble remembering good old Bill Wilson's last name simply because we know several other Bills.

Roman orators of many centuries ago had extremely elaborate systems of memory *loci*. Undoubtedly one of the greatest mnemonists of all time was Peter of Ravenna, who lived around 1490 and wrote the most widely known textbook about memory. Peter used the *loci* system and geared his book not to scholars but to common people. Like Simonides, Peter advised his readers to select a quiet place with few people around to build a sequence of *loci*, a nearly empty church, for instance. He described going to this or that church three or four times and systematically walking about inside and memorizing the sequence of places. Wherever he traveled he visited local churches and so expanded his *loci* system until he had reportedly built it up into a sequence of over 100,000 places! According to Frances Yates in her excellent book, *The Art of Memory*, it is said that he could repeat from memory 200 speeches or sayings of Cicero, 300 sayings of the philosophers, and 20,000 legal points, among other things. Before leaving *loci* as a system of mnemonics, we should mention the role of the great religious scholar Thomas Aquinas in preserving the imagery system of memory. You'll recall from an earlier chapter that St. Thomas said that we cannot understand thoughts without images of them. The memory-training system of St. Thomas was just about the same as that originally invented by Simonides. It was because of the work of St. Thomas that Simonides's mnemonic system of imagery was revived and given a permanent *locus* in the hall of memory.

LULL'S VERBAL MNEMONICS

At the time St. Thomas was teaching his memory-training system, another scholar, Ramon Lull, was developing a new system of his own. Lull's memory system was an extremely complex one that depended on religious and philosophical ideas rather than on graphic images. For example, Lull began with nine Names for God: Goodness, Greatness, Eternity, Power, Wisdom, Will, Virtue, Truth, and Glory. Each of these Names of God could be used on nine different levels, or "steps to the House of Wisdom." Climbing the steps from the bottom, in order, we would find: (1) the Virtues and the Arts and Sciences; (2) the Four Basic Elements: Earth, Air, Fire, and Water; (3) Plants; (4) Animals; (5) Imagination; (6) Man; (7) Stars; (8) Angels; (9) God. Again, Lull's system is much too complex to be easily useful to us today. It is mentioned here because it was the first verbal mnemonic system to be widely used.

Among the simplest verbal mnemonic systems is organizing the material to be remembered into rhymes. In spelling, for instance, we are taught that the letter **i** always comes before **e** except after **c**, as in the words bel**ie**ve and rece**i**ve. Chances are that you know the rhyme that helps us remember how many days each month has: "Thirty days hath September, April, June, and November; all the rest have thirty-one excepting February alone, which has twenty-eight days clear, and twenty-nine in each leap year." Nearly all rhyming memory schemes have two things in common: (1) They have a built-in guarantee to work (if you remember the rhyme) because if you forget part of the rhyme, or get part of it wrong, the words lose their proper rhythm or the lines fail to rhyme, and so tell you that something is wrong. (2) Usually, to recall a single bit of information stored in rhyme, you have to repeat the whole rhyme to retrieve the bit you want. This is like using a tape in a computer memory bank. The entire tape must be run through to isolate the individual bit of information wanted. For example, using the above rhyme, how many days are there in May? As clumsy as this system may at first appear, it has been around for a long time for one very good reason. It works. So don't overlook the use of rhymes, *of your own invention,* to memorize things that are important for you to have at the "tip of your memory."

RHYMING, IMAGERY, AND ASSOCIATION

Although rhyming is involved in the following mnemonic scheme, it is used only to help you memorize a base list of ten objects. Once you have memorized the list you then put it to use by associating visual images. Here's how it works. First, memorize the following list:

> One is a bun
> Two is a shoe
> Three is a tree
> Four is a door
> Five is a hive
> Six is sticks
> Seven is heaven
> Eight is a gate
> Nine is a line
> Ten is a hen

It shouldn't take you more than two minutes to memorize this rhyming list. Once you have it memorized you can then put it to work to help you remember dates, telephone numbers, and just about anything else. For example, say that you want to memorize the number 10785. Here's how. First associate the numbers 10, 7, 8, and 5 with the key words hen, heaven, gate, hive. Next, make up a story:

I'll never forget that wonderful pet **hen** I had. She was so good, always woke us up at just the right time in the morning and had the habit of laying Easter eggs. She was so good that when she died she went to **heaven** and was greeted at the **gate** by cheering groups of her relatives, all of whom had been done in by Colonel Sanders. Then she was ushered to her new home, a huge dome-shaped enclosure. "How strange," she said, "I never expected that I, a hen, would one day live in a **hive**."

Although this may seem to be the long way around to remember 10785, it is much quicker than the unaided method of repetitious rehearsal. Depending on how lively an imagination you have, it shouldn't take more than five or ten seconds to put together such a comic strip of images. If the number 10785 that you want to remember happens to be the house number of your new friend, Mary, all you have to do is think of Mary as your pet hen and you'll be unlikely to forget the number. Again, this system may strike you as being silly. But the point is that it works, and largely because it *is* silly.

THE NUMBER-CONSONANT ALPHABET

Courses in how to improve your memory are fairly common today. Most of them use a system called the number-consonant alphabet, which in one form or another has been around for nearly five hundred years. This may strike you as a rather difficult system. Actually it isn't as hard as it seems at first, and once you get the hang of it you'll find that it works very well and can be impressively fast. The first thing you must do is memorize the number-consonant table, memorizing the *sounds* of the letters associated with the numbers 0 through 9, not memorizing visual images of the letters. That is important, and you'll soon understand why.

ARTICLE 6 TABLE 1

Number	Letters	Sounds	How to Remember
0	s, c	ess, zzz	Zero starts with z
1	t, d, th	t	The vertical bar of a t looks like a figure 1.
2	n	en	A written n has two strokes.
3	m	em	A written m has three strokes.
4	r	r	Four ends in an r.
5	l	el	L is 50 in Roman numerals.
6	sh, j, ch, g	sh, j, soft g	She juggles; she charges.
7	k, g, ng	k, hard c and hard g	G is seventh letter in alphabet.
8	f, v, ph	ef, vee, ph	Written f looks like long 8.
9	b, p	b, p	Both b and p can be turned into 9s.

Memorizing this table, concentrating on giving each number the *sounds* and not the shapes of their associated letters, will take you longer than memorizing the "One is a bun" list. But don't be discouraged; you can do it, and more easily than you may think. Again, rehearse it. Now let's see how the number-consonant system can be used.

Suppose that you want to memorize the telephone number 627-1472. Translating the numbers into the sounds that we find most useful gives us *shnngdrgn*, which in its raw form isn't much help. But when we do a further translation into sh-n-ng d-r-g-n, and fill in the spaces with vowels, we have a meaningful and graphic image—a "shining dragon," a convenient mnemonic for a telephone number. Again, the system works, and is quite fast once you have mastered it. It would be a good idea for you to practice translating twenty or thirty words into their number equivalents simply to get used to associating numbers with sounds. For example, "bun" translates into 93; "tong" into 17; "table" into 195; and "jel" into 65.

Now on your own use the number-consonant alphabet as a mnemonic for this long number. When you have finished turn the page to see the mnemonic I came up with.

5 9 8 3 7 8 2 9 1 0

The sounds of words in combination with their shapes have been used as a mnemonic technique for teaching young children to read in English schools. The story of Sammy Snake and the Hairy Hat Man shown on the opposite page is an example.

REDUCTION MNEMONICS

Still another mnemonic system is one called *reduction mnemonics*, in which you reduce a relatively large body of material into a shorter form. You then invent a clever way of memorizing the shorter form, which on recall you can then elaborate back into the original form you wanted to

 for Sammy Snake    for <u>S</u>ammy <u>S</u>nake

This snake slithers and slides along making a soft hissing sound in words, like this "sssss." His name is Sammy Snake.

Sam sits hissing in the sun.

To *Write* This Letter:
Start at Sammy Snake's head and stroke him all the way down to the tip of his tail. Sammy says it feels good when you do that. (He does *not* like people to draw him starting at his tail. That makes him very cross.)

 for hairy hat man

 for Hairy Hat Man doing a Handstand with His Hat on

The Hairy Hat Man hates hearing noise, so he never speaks above a whisper. This is why all you will ever hear him say in words is "hhh." He is whispering "hhh" for "Hat Man." You may wonder what he is doing going about with bare feet all of the time. Actually he never wears shoes because they make too much noise. You see, he doesn't even want to hear the sound of his own footsteps. (In a few words, he makes no sound at all because he likes peace and quiet so much.) Can you hear him whispering "hhh" in these words?

He has a hundred hats.

The Hairy Hat Man always hurries along in the Reading Direction (this way →) like nearly everyone else in Letter Land.

The Snake is told "Shhh" by the Hat Man.

Sammy Snake is also one of the Hairy Hat Man's pets, and the Hat Man takes good care of him. The only trouble is that Sammy Snake loves hissing. None of the other Letter People minds his hissing sound when he is beside them in a word, but the Hairy Hat Man hates noise. So when Sammy Snake comes up behind *him* in a word the Hairy Hat Man turns back angrily and says to him, "Shhhhh." In fact, the Hat Man says "Shhhh" so loudly that Sammy stops hissing right away and tries to say "Shhhh," too.

This shop sells fresh fish

This mnemonic system was designed to teach reading and writing to English school children. It is from L. Wendon, The Pictogram System: Set One (Cambridge, England: Barton–Pictogram Supplies).

memorize in the first place. For example, the way student pilots are taught to remember (for their written exam) the five documents they must carry with them in the airplane is to remember the word ARROW. "Always have an ARROW with you in the airplane."

A   Airworthiness certificate of the airplane
R   Registration of the airplane
R   Radio transmitter license
O   Operating limitations of the airplane
W   Weight and balance data

You can remember the names of the five Great Lakes by using the reduction mnemonic HOMES and imagining the lakes as your personal home.

H   Huron
O   Ontario
M   Michigan
E   Erie
S   Superior

Astronomy students learn the spectral classes of stars by a system called *elaboration mnemonics*. Here you invent a longer, but meaningful, expression for the short one you want to memorize. For example, the seven major spectral classes of stars, in order, are O, B, A, F, G, K, M. The elaboration mnemonic for this otherwise meaningless string of letters has long been "**O** Be **A** Fine **G**irl and **K**iss **M**e." Physics students also use this technique when they remember the order of colors in the visual spectrum: R (red), O (orange), Y (yellow), G (green), B (blue), I (indigo), and V (violet). The mnemonic is "**R**ichard **O**f **Y**ork **G**ains **B**attles **I**n **V**ain." Baddeley reports a combination rhyming and elaboration technique that enabled him to memorize the value of *pi* to the first 20 places:

My mnemonic for the long number on page 92.

LaP oF MaGoo FiT PeTS

Pie
I wish I could remember *pi*.
"Eureka," cried the great inventor,
"Christmas pudding, Christmas pie,
Is the problem's very centre."

Baddeley says that he never had trouble remembering the silly verse, but he kept forgetting how to put it to work to give the answer! Actually, it's simple—just count the number of letters in each word: Pie = 3; I = 1; wish = 4, and so on to give: 3.14158265358979323846.

SUBSTITUTION MNEMONICS

The altitude of Mt. Fuji, in Japan, is 12,365 feet. How do I remember this? Easy. I remember Mt. Fuji as Calendar Mountain, which has 12 months and 365 days. There is a seemingly endless way of using *substitution mnemonics*, or substituting words rich in images for people's names, for instance. The trick—and it is a trick, but one that works—is somehow to make the face or some other feature of the person remind you of an absurd name substituted for the person's real name. The instant you are introduced, a graphic substitute for the person's name must flash into your thoughts and be associated with some prominent feature. For example, you are introduced to Mr. Carpenter, who happens to be a very fat man. Immediately you picture him in baggy work clothes inching his way up a tiny and shaky ladder on his way to finish the roof of the new house he is building. Or you must remember to admire the stripes on the sleeve of Mr. Sargent, who happens to remind you of a tough drill sergeant.

Those names are easy, you may say. What about Lawsen, or Oxford, or Razzano, or Dobinski? Let's take them one at a time, and most likely you already have your own substitution mnemonic for at least two of them, I see Ms. Lawsen accompanied wherever she goes by her tiny **son** carrying a great **law** book. Whoops! I must remember not to trip over her little son.

Mr. Oxford has two tufts of hair that remind me of the horns of an ox, so I picture this **ox** of a man **ford**ing a river with his head held high to keep his hair-horns from getting wet. Next I am introduced to Mrs. Razzano, who happens to have a small mole on her neck. It reminds me of a raisin and I immediately call her Miss **Rais**in-of-the-Year (Latin for "year" being **ano**).

"And this is Mr. Dobinski," my hostess says as she presents this man with a long face that reminds me of a horse. So immediately he becomes old **Dobbin,** not hitched to a sleigh, but **ski**ing wildly down a mountainside. Again, the trick here is to find some distinguishing feature, or even item of clothing or jewelry, to combine with your substitution mnemonic.

With practice you will find it becoming easier and easier to use this system of remembering names. And you'll be pleasantly surprised at how well it works the very first time you put it to use.

Substitution mnemonics can be used in many situations other than in remembering names. For example, you can easily memorize the capitals of various states. The capital of Maine is Augusta. So I picture a windy Maine coast and my friend saying, "**A gust, huh**? It's more like a hurricane." And what about Massachusetts? I once worked in its capital for a publisher and remember that my **boss** weighed a **ton**. See what you come up with for substitute mnemonics for the following state capitals:

State	Capital
Connecticut	Hartford
Delaware	Dover
Illinois	Springfield
Kansas	Topeka
Kentucky	Frankfort
Oregon	Salem
South Dakota	Pierre
Washington	Olympia
Wyoming	Cheyenne

(If you didn't come up with *Shy Anne* for Wyoming, go back to

Go and don't collect $200.)

You can also use substitution mnemonics for memorizing vocabulary lists for foreign languages, or just pinning down that illusive Chinese word that you can never seem to remember when you want it. You can remember *avocat* which is the French word for "lawyer" as an **avocado-**lawyer pleading a case in court. And the French words *père* and *mère* for "father" and "mother": I can throw a **pear** much **farther** than I can throw my **mother**, who is a **mare**. Or the Japanese word *yama* for "mountain" can be thought of as a **yam** the size of a mountain. Substitution mnemonics applied to memorizing foreign words and phrases has proven to be a very effective way of firmly planting a word or phrase in your short-term memory and keeping it there long enough for eventual transfer into your long-term memory through rehearsal (actual use). After that you may no longer have need for the substitute mnemonic, but chances are that you'll retain it.

ASSOCIATION WORD LISTS

Association word lists also are an effective and commonly used mnemonic system. As in the *loci* system of Simonides you must memorize a list of key words, or "peg" words. You can, of course, make the list as long as you wish. In the *loci* system, you'll recall, the list is easy to memorize because it is based on a sequence of places in a room or building well known to you. In word association lists, a different method is used. The words are carefully chosen so that the mnemonist has no trouble immediately knowing what word precedes and what word follows any given word in the list. Here's how such a list can be made up. Again, if you decide to use this system, invent your own list because it will work better for you than a list made up by someone else.

I made up the following list in less than five minutes simply to demonstrate how the system works.

first base	soil	milk	bull's eye	canoe
fox	field	kitten	target	paddle
chicken	grass	dog	straw	tennis
egg	plant	setter	soda	net
seed	milkweed	point	water	fish
corn	cow	tip	lake	(etc.)
		arrow		

It is not a particularly good list but is good enough to serve as a guide. First base seemed a good starting point, and a fox sitting on first base seemed silly enough to get the association sequence going. Foxes like chickens; chickens lay eggs; eggs are a kind of seed; corn is a real seed; corn grows in the soil; soil occurs in fields; grass grows in fields; and so on. The working power of such a list depends entirely on how cleverly you are able to establish associations between consecutive words in the list. Again, as with a long list of *loci,* it is a good idea to use some technique to make every fifth or tenth item on the list stand out so that you can keep track of the items you want to remember and then recall in any demanded sequence.

It isn't hard to see how easily such a word-association list can be generated. But then it should be worked on carefully to make it as easy as possible to memorize. Once it has been memorized it can be used exactly the same way the *loci* list is used. As you experiment with these mnemonic techniques try both the *loci* system and the word association system to find out which works better for you.

According to Gordon H. Bower, a psychologist and investigator into the art and science of memory, you should keep several essential principles in mind as you draw up a word association list and use it:

1. Both the words forming your base list and the items to be remembered by association must be translated into striking visual images.

2. The images formed by a given base-list word and the word associated with it and to be memorized must interact so that the two form a single image (remember the superintendent

sitting on the plant stand?)

3. The base-list words should be drawn up by the mnemonist.

4. Sometimes it is possible to associate more than one item to be remembered with a single base-list word, but such multiple words should form but a single image, such as a *cow* eating *grass* in a *field*. Efficiency of the system drops off when separate and multiple images are attached too often to base-list words.

5. It is not a good idea to choose words for the base list that are similar to other words in the list.

Quick, what was the street address of your new friend, Mary?

THE ART OF "CHUNKING"

Psychologist: How do you play that piece from memory?

Pianist: (After thinking hard for a while) I haven't the slightest idea, really. I sort of hear the melody in my head and my fingers just seem to know what to do.

Often it is not easy to explain how we remember to perform a certain act, or recall a series of numbers or words, a feat which to us may seem quite unspectacular but which to someone else might seem quite remarkable. Recall the mnemonist V.P. who showed unusual mnemonic abilities at a very early age. Most of us have a memory span of about seven digits or seven words. But V.P. could easily and quickly memorize as many as seventeen digits and did not find the task difficult. A. C. Aitken also was able to memorize long strings of numbers. Both did, quite naturally, what many professional mnemonists have taught themselves to do over a period of time, the art of *chunking*.

Say that someone with an average memory span of seven items is given the following sequence of seventeen numbers to memorize:

14921952375193539

As V.P. was accustomed to doing in such cases when a long series of numbers was read off to him at the rate of one number a second, he instantly found patterns and accordingly broke down the long series into three or five smaller groups, or "chunks." Each smaller group of numbers held a specific meaning for him, a meaning that easily enabled him to remember the entire sequence. For example, the above sequence of seventeen digits might have been regrouped, or chunked, into five units, like this:

1492	1952	375	1935	39
Columbus sailed to America	Year I returned from the Korean War	House number when I lived on Elm St.	Year we moved to Portland	Age of my sister

Psychologists say that our "chunking capacity" is the same as our memory span; that is, from five to nine items of information, one item being a number or a letter or a group of numbers or a group of letters (a word). If each number in the sequence 3 5 8 2 9 7 0 represents one chunk, then we have just about filled up our average chunking capacity of seven chunks. But now we see two meaningful patterns in the series; 358 and 2970. What we have done is reduce our memory task from one of remembering seven chunks to one of remembering only two chunks. Since our average chunking capacity is seven, then we have room for five additional chunks. Any of those chunks may be made up of one item or two or more related items. For some reason our memory accepts each chunk, no matter how large, as a single item. For instance, memorizing pi to twenty places by using a single technique would represent one chunk.

Chunking has been studied in great detail by psychologists and has proven to be a very effective way of enlarging our short-term memory capacity. So your cleverness at chunking determines how much you can pack into your short-term memory and retain there long enough for rehearsal and transfer into your long-term memory. Let's consider another example of chunking, this time with letters and words. Admittedly this is a contrived example, but it makes the point of how to make chunking work for you on more than one level. The task is to remember the following sequence of letters, either forward or backward:

CATDOGRATBICYCLEPOLICEVETNURSESTRETCHERBEARERS

Since you (most likely) have a normal chunking capacity of up to nine items, you are able to memorize the maximum of the first nine letters:

$$1 \ \ 2 \ \ 3 \ \ 4 \ \ 5 \ \ 6 \ \ 7 \ \ 8 \ \ 9$$
$$C \ \ A \ \ T \ \ D \ \ O \ \ G \ \ R \ \ A \ \ T$$

It is not difficult to regroup and reduce those nine chunks into chunks:

$$1 \qquad 2 \qquad 3$$
$$CAT \ \ DOG \ \ RAT$$

You now have room for six additional chunks. You can add B I C Y C L, like this,

$$1 \qquad 2 \qquad 3 \qquad + \ \ 1 \ \ 2 \ \ 3 \ \ 4 \ \ 5 \ \ 6 = 9$$
$$CAT \ \ DOG \ \ RAT \qquad B \ \ I \ \ C \ \ Y \ \ C \ \ L$$

or with a little work you see an easy way to cluster a larger number of the remaining letters into chunks, to give a total of nine chunks:

1	2	3
CAT	DOG	RAT
1	2	3
+ BICYCLE	POLICE	VET
4	5	6
+ NURSE	STRETCHER	BEARERS
= 9 chunks		

So by regrouping, or rechunking, you have managed to contain the entire sequence of letters in your normal chunking capacity. And now by the use of images that you put into action you almost instantly lock the entire sequence of forty-six letters firmly into your short-term memory: While walking down the street you see a dog and cat fight. At the same time you see a rat riding past the scene on a bicycle. Because the rat is speeding, he is being chased by a policeman. Then in the distance you see a veterinarian running to patch up the wounds of the dog and cat. Right behind him is a nurse, also running to the scene, and behind her are stretcher bearers to take the animals to the hospital. Again, this is a very effective system which has been tested by psychologists attempting to find out more about how our memory works.

Chunking, they tell us, is a reliable way of improving our short-term memory spans. Chunking proved to be an important technique in the memories of both S and V.P. V.P., however, seems not to have relied strongly on visual-image mnemonics as did S. Instead, V.P. relied mostly on verbal mnemonics. When he memorized a table of numbers he did not "photograph" the table, as S did. Instead, V.P. memorized the numbers in each row of the table as a series of dates, then he remembered what he had done on each date. While such a system apparently works well for some people, there is no guarantee that it will work well for you. The important thing is that you understand the principle of chunking, then experiment until you hit on a method of chunking that does work well for you.

Don't overlook the art of chunking people, such as the couples Ted and Alice, Wilma and Paul, and so on. Recalling the name of one person of the pair usually suggests the name of the other person.

Master chess players, by the way, are able to take a quick look at a chess board and then without again looking at the board tell you where every piece was located at the time they looked. They do this very simply by chunking the various individual pieces into meaningful clusters. So a total of four-teen individual pieces is quickly grouped as two chunks, one of five pieces beside another of nine pieces. This compaction of fourteen items into two chunks puts less stress on the short-term memory, and at the same time makes room for ad-ditional information to be temporarily stored.

MEMORY PILLS

They are called "smart pills," "mind food," "intelligence boosters," and "creative expanders." They are drugs that are supposed to improve your memory and speed up the learning process. At least one popular magazine has listed about a dozen such drugs and has taken on the role of physician by prescribing how much of each drug to take over a specified time. Your brain is a very precious thing—to you—and to risk damaging it by following quack advice about tak-ing dangerous habit-forming drugs with known, or in some cases unknown, side effects, would be ill-advised in the ex-treme. There is no harm in reading about these so-called in-telligence boosters, but there may be very real harm in experimenting with them without the benefit of your family physician's guidance. No matter what a friend or "research scientist" may advise you about taking memory pills, don't, at least not without first discussing the matter with a physician.

It should be obvious by now that memory is not under the control of any supernatural powers. It is true that some people are born with better memories than others. When such people are aware of their above-average ability they may decide to set about improving their memories by adopting any number of mnemonic techniques. People with normal, or even below normal, memories also can improve their ability to remember dates, names, faces, or anything else they attempt to. The se-cret is to reorganize a body of information into compartments that you can later search and from which you can retrieve whatever items you may want at the moment. Proper organization, or structuring and associating, are the key words here. So be confident that you can learn to use your memory *much* more efficiently than you are using it now. But you will have to work at it. You can regard each mnemonic technique as a very efficient shortcut to the sometimes laborious process of rehearsal that might not always work as well or as fast as you would like it to. You will find that a good memory means paying attention, concentrating, and organizing in a meaningful way whatever information you want to remember.

INDEX

Roy A.